Amazing Trace

A Sister's Journal

Karen West

With Ginni Michek
"Ginni" Poems by Merissa Kelley

Amazing Trace

Original Artwork by Laura Dameron

Poetry by Merissa Kelley

ISBN: 978-1-4303-0242-1

This journal is lovingly dedicated to all breast cancer survivors worldwide and to those who fought bravely and won the golden tiara in Heaven.

God Bless you.
www.tracesjourney.com

Introduction

My name is Karen West. I am the Midday Personality at country station 97-3 The Eagle in Virginia Beach, VA. This is my account of my sister's battle with breast cancer and her active role in my own life changing experiences. Ginni has taught (and is still teaching) me how to see blessings in the midst of tragedy. That's a difficult job. Especially if one is mourning a loss of a marriage, a job, or even a loved one. Amazingly, she was able to find at least one blessing at the heart of each trial. She wrote her thoughts almost daily, and in her last year, recorded her daily blessings in red ink. How does one find these wonderful things in the course of cancer, the death of friends and a divorce? She did. Hopefully, my little book will help us all find a little bit of peace just like she did, even when we feel all is hopeless.

By no means do I claim to be a writer. Ginni's words were considerably more eloquent than mine and you will see the distinctions with her journal entries. (Included in bold, italic). Yes, I have always dreamed of being a writer like J.K. Rowling, but I gave up after reading the Harry Potter series. (Some people are gifted with great imaginations!)   Ah, but this journal is not intended to be the "Great American Novel." Its purpose is to fulfill what Ginni asked of me; to be a blessing for others.

Ginni believed that having cancer made her a better person. Amazingly, she adored her new outlook on life. Her faith and spiritual well-being became stronger even as her body grew weaker. She was definitely unique; finding good things in the worst situations.

"But how did I get here? And how much further do I have to go? Can I tell you what God has shared with my heart in the past year? The first thing that I have accepted is that this cancer is His will for my life. And if it's His will, how can I be against it? And as stupid as it sounds, I wouldn't change a thing. Don't get me wrong, I don't wish I had cancer, but I do and if I had to do it over, I would do it again. I'm not the same me as before and I like this me better. YIKES!   I've also learned that today is truly that proverbial GIFT. It's mine and I can't give it away and if I don't use it, it's wasted and I don't get it back. WHOA! WHAT A CONCEPT. And once I learned and accepted that, I learned to STAY IN TODAY."

"Stay in today." It took losing her to realize that tomorrow is not ours…yet. Tomorrow is a gift, but this very moment is ours. It shouldn't be wasted in anger or trivial issues; but to be cherished somehow, someway. From Ginni's journal: *"Never allow yourself to complain about anything – not even the weather. Never picture yourself in any other circumstance or someplace else. That is true contentment."* "Stay in today" doesn't mean "don't plan for tomorrow." It means, don't let tomorrow's worries interfere with the present.

Ginni did not want to waste one precious moment. She wrote in her journals regularly and took photographs nearly every-day. (I can only recall a couple of times when she didn't have a camera readily available.) She always wanted special memories "on hand" on days when she was feeling particularly "puny", as she referred to it. Fond memories helped her through tough moments; thus motivating her to "stay in today."

Ginni requested that I journal my experiences as a care-giver, a stem cell donor and a sister. I remember that day fondly. On March 5th, 2005, we were staying at the Navy Lodge across the street from National Institutes of health. In preparation for stem cell donation, over the course of 5 days, I injected myself twice daily with Neupogen, a drug to boost my white blood count. The more my body produced the extra cells, the sicker I got. That was a good sign because it meant the shots were working. I could barely move. My head was pounding, I had fever and my body was sore. I lay in the bed with ice packs on my head.

As Ginni was writing her thoughts for the day, she glanced over to see if I was writing as well. "You should document your experiences, sis." I told her I did not have the energy or the men-tality at that moment. I didn't tell her that I've always been too darn lazy to write a grocery list, much less my thoughts. She asked, "How are people going to learn from your experiences unless you write them down so you can remember them?" I chuckled, "Oh, I'll never forget this day, that's for sure." She walked to my bedside and began sorting through my travel bag.   "Your experiences could benefit someone else later. Write them down. I bet that journal I bought for you is still empty, dork!" She was right. "Okay, I will." She was skeptical of my agreement. "Pick it up now and start writing while you still remember everything. Write about how your body feels from the injections. Write how you feel about the clinical trial. Write about everything, sis. Me … you … the cancer. Others may find comfort in your story."

I moaned as I sat up on the side of the bed. I slowly stood up and hobbled to the little kitchenette for a drink. Ginni followed. I hugged her and we wept. "Ginni, I don't think I've ever been in this much pain before, but I want you to know just how worth it you are. You are so worth this, and much more. I love you so much." She hugged me tighter. "You're doing so well, sis. Hang in there. You are doing so much better than I would have." I knew that wasn't true. She was giving cancer a run for its money, and had been doing so for over 10 years. We were still embracing when I looked up and said, "God, please help me stop feeling so sorry for myself *right now*." At that very moment (I swear this happened), the tiny smoke alarm in the kitchenette started blaring. We weren't cooking anything. It just went off by itself! We both backed away and stared at each other in amazement. "Are you still feeling sorry for yourself?" she asked. "Um, no. Prayer answered. I believe I'm over myself now." Was it an answer to prayer? I believe so. I have kept a journal ever since that moment.

I have included some pages at the end of each chapter so you may take note of your blessings in times of troubles, and if you would like to share them with me, I would love to hear from you! Drop me a note anytime: Karen@tracesjourney.com.

Yours,
Karen

Karen: "Hey! How did *you* get *two* Barbies?"
Ginni: "I *do* recall I whooped your butt for them."

Ginni: "Hey Toby! Wrong camera dork!"

Acknowledgments

I thank God for His love and all the wonderful people He has blessed me with:

- My husband Jim for your love and understanding during my time of grief.

- My children Laura, Allison and Gabrielle for making sure I never have a dull moment.

- Margot McKenney Bunger and Sandy Dunn for allowing me to be part of your lives. And for loving me as one of your own.

- All my co-workers at Max Media of Hampton Roads for being my cheerleaders.

- My grandparents, Henry & Estelle Huey and Aunt Joan Specht picking up where Mom left off. There are not enough "thank yous" in the world.

- Wayne, Joannie and Ken, my wonderful brothers and sister for all of the teasing.

- The Ya-Ya Sisterhood for taking Ginni and me under your wing.

- Chris, Katy and Jesse … your Mom was the best and she raised such beautiful children. Always know that she is so proud.

And of course, to our beloved Ginni.

I love all of you so much!

Table of Contents

Lessons Along The Way

I've learned a lot of lessons, as the years have rolled on by
I know sometimes I won't get answers to all my questions why
Every time that I'm in doubt, it's to my knees I go
For just because it "looks" real good, doesn't make it so

I've learned it's folly to put plans in motion and then ask God to
bless them
For the end result of that course of action, is usually chaos and
mayhem
I've learned forgiveness is more for yourself than the person you
need to forgive
It's a conscious decision, that's not based on feelings and the only
way to live

I've learned there's nothing here on earth that compares with
God's sweet grace
He knows I need an unlimited amount, to keep running in the race
My lack of faith does not decrease God's ability to answer prayer
I know He loves me in spite of myself, He's good, He's just and
fair

Trusting and waiting are two of the toughest areas in which to
yield
We like control and giving that up is like letting down our shield
You can't change people...that's up to God...and only if they
submit
And the possibility you need some changes, is something that's
hard to admit

Sometimes it's hard to see the good in the middle of a test
You get so tired of pressing in and you'd like a little rest
Trials are tests and tests can teach, but you must choose to learn
To keep your faith in the fiery furnace and not give up and burn

Tears are cleansing, music heals and laughter brings release
Praise will lift you, prayer sustains and trust will give you peace
Joy is inside, hope endures and faith is a lifestyle choice
The Word is truth, Heaven is real and I know my Savior's voice

So when I start to question why a trial is so intense
I must remember, He's very close and preparing my defense
By His grace and by His mercy, I can face each passing day
And know He's working for my good...in the lessons along the way

© 2002 Merissa Lee Kelley

"It was a dark and stormy night..." I can just about hear Ginni chuckle, "Dork" because I began our story with a "Snoopy-ism." "Webster's dictionary describes "Dork" as a "stupid or ridiculous person." Ginni said the word was *her* version of TV character Fred G. Sanford's "You big dummy!" I would do almost anything to hear her say that "endearing" name once more. As far as I'm concerned, it is the most beautiful name on the planet because it made her laugh. Don't get me wrong. Not just anybody can get away with calling me "Dork." With her, it carried a different tone. It was her reply to my teasing her as I often did. Most of the time, those little jokes helped her forget, if only temporarily, her serious issues. Ginni passed away of breast cancer April 8, 2005 after nearly 11 years of fighting.

Every once in awhile, someone asks me when I plan to write about my sister's life with breast cancer. "You two have such a beautiful story," or "I have a loved one who is suffering breast cancer. How do you hold it together so well?" Being in the media, I have learned to "hold it together" for the airwaves, and cry in the privacy of my own home. If I were asked last year, I would've said I will never attempt to write it. After all, the only thing I've ever written was radio commercial scripts, and, I was certainly in no position to remember all of the good times when the loss was so new.

I'm flattered that people are interested in our story. If I had attempted to write it right after Ginni died, I would have spent months staring at blank paper. Blank, just like my mind. Grief had me by the toenails and I spent more than a year going through the motions of existence. Until one day I woke up and remembered that the world was *still* turning and I was *still* on it. I had to take some time to learn to live all over again before I could commit the time to this project.

As I'm writing this, I am awaiting my own test results for breast cancer. On Halloween 2006, I had my annual mammogram.

On Thursday November 2nd, I received a call from the lab with news of a significant concern. Perhaps I shouldn't have planned my mammo on the scariest day of the year, huh? My primary care physician requested a closer look at a suspicious lump in the upper right quadrant of my right breast. I had problems there before. Two years ago, I had a benign lump removed. For the last couple of weeks, I have been experiencing tenderness in that area. I am scheduled for another mammogram and an ultrasound on Monday, November 6. I don't know how my story is going to end. I just pray that either way, I'll be able to see God in control, just like Ginni did.

I have accepted that it's going to be one of two diagnoses. Either I'm going to have breast cancer or I'm not. If I don't, I'm planning a huge party. Cartwheels and all! Nevertheless, I'll remain aware that I am at risk. If I do have it, well, it will be a different kind of party. Ginni-style. Boas, tiaras and junk food on chemo day. I have the choice of fighting or not, and I choose to whoop some cancer butt!

Ginni showed me how to be tough. I was ordinarily the one who avoided all conflicts, but she took them head-on. She loved this quote from television minister Joyce Meyer: "You can't go over it, you can't go under it. You have to go through it," referring to life's obstacles. Ginni taught me, by example, how to live each day as a gift, and she offered advice on how to deal with worry: "Take it one day at a time ... and if one day is too much, take it one hour at a time ... and if that is too much, take it one minute at a time." Today, I've been taking quite a few "minute" intervals, but I find it has been easier to deal with the situation this way; so I can, as Ginni says, "stay in today."

I seriously wish I had her *right now* to talk me through this. Fortunately, I have her journals to read for comfort. Each day she thanked God for loving her and providing her, even when she was experiencing pain. Ginni's written words confirm that she was truly a loving and genuine human being. Those years between her diagnosis and death were spent encouraging and loving others unconditionally, and God rewarded her for trusting in Him. I watched her leave this earth and she left it so peacefully and beautifully, it was no question that angels escorted her Home.   It was as though God said, "Well done, my daughter, Ginni. Well done."

She was known as "Trace" in the cyber-world. A name she adopted from one of her favorite country music artists, Trace Adkins. She was born Virginia Estelle Turpin, named for both grandmothers. I called her Ginni. During her last three years, I often referred to her as "Ms. Monk" because of one or two obsessive-compulsive traits she had much like the TV detective "Adrian Monk." She enjoyed that moniker, often taking her "compulsions" over the edge just to get a laugh.

We were just 14 months apart. Although I was only a toddler, remarkably, I remember the day she was born. It was a cloudy day on October 10, 1962. I was in Arlington with my mom and dad visiting with my grandfather whom I met for the first time. Mom was due to have Ginni at any minute.   I believe the reason she risked the trip from Newport News is because she thought Ginni would be at least 2 weeks late, just as I was.

I remember my parents leaving the house in a hurry, and I stayed behind with this man I believed was a "big scary" stranger. I recall sobbing so hard I made myself sick. I assume it was from separation anxiety as I was not even two years old yet. As I climbed the stairs with my "big scary-man" grandpa, I remember throwing up on my new black patent leather shoes. He quickly scooped me up and raced to the bathroom. I was frightened. I thought he was angry because I had just wrecked the carpet on the stairs, but to my surprise, he wasn't angry with me at all. He gently cleaned my face and my clothing and took me to the guest room so I could lie down for a nap.

My next memory is sitting at the dinner table with "big scary-man" and dad. I was in a makeshift high chair, which was just a typical wooden high back chair with a couple of thick phone books in the seat. There was a small cup of 7-up and a bowl of green beans in front of me. I recall how good the soft drink felt on my stomach and it wasn't long before I was able to eat every green bean in that little bowl. My grandpa smiled. He was no longer "big scary-man" because he helped me recover from my tantrum-induced illness. He said Mom was coming home with a "gift" *just* for me and I would cherish it forever. I don't remember exactly what I thought it was, but I'm sure at that age I would have been happy with a cardboard box.

I remember being safely at home and watching the little "doll" in the bassinet. I don't remember how much time had passed before we were back in my comfortable surroundings, but I do remember it was the first time I had laid eyes on my "gift." I loved it, just like Grandpa said. She looked like me and smelled pretty; like baby powder. Mom introduced her as "your baby", and from that moment on, she was my baby, my punching bag, my confidante, the thorn in my side, my savior and my best friend.

Growing up, we were your typical sisters. We played well together and fought until we drew blood. I was the more girly of the two so most of the time I lost the "fistfights", though sometimes I took a "dive" just so she would leave me alone! She was the tomboy. Most of her toddler and adolescent years were spent in stitches or casts. If it was risky, Ginni tried it. Whether she was climbing on the roof of the neighbor's garage and jumping off, or building bicycle "ramps" from heaps of boxes and plywood, she often referred to herself as the "Evel Knevel" of 49th Street, Newport News. If 911 was available on speed dial in the 70's, our mother would have programmed it on every phone in the house and labeled it "Ginni." We kept the doctors in ER employed, that's for sure!

Today, as I am sitting here listening to my 14 and 17-year old daughters squabble over a pair of "skinny" jeans, I can recall a crazy teenage brawl Ginni and I had. It was over a "cute" pink and blue striped cowl-necked sweater. One that ended with both of us sprawled out across my bed throwing punches, pulling hair and slipping in a few choice words. I believe the expression "I hate you" may have crossed our lips a few times. Baby sister Joannie was crouched in a corner terrified that our grandmother would enter at any moment and punish the whole bunch of us. Poor Joannie. She was usually guilty by association. Nevertheless, I believe Joannie could have been spared had she just escaped downstairs to have breakfast instead of staying to witness the first round of "Early Morning Smack down."

I would like to assume I won that battle, but I didn't. Ginni's tomboyish character gave her the advantage. I, more than likely, did not want to break a nail. Even then, at 15 with her perfectly coiffed Farrah Fawcett 'do, a slight touch of pink on her naturally high cheekbones and carefully applied clear Bonne Belle lip gloss, she still managed to beat the crap out of me and not get a hair out of place! As suspected, Grandma grounded us for that 70's version of the "Jerry Springer Show", but Ginni did not care. She got the "prize" … the sweater that was given to me by "Santa Granddaddy" just a month before. Fortunately as we got older, we stopped fighting over clothing. Instead, she just rifled through my closet and "borrowed" what she liked. "We're sisters and sisters always share," was her excuse. "Sure" I thought, as I reclaimed my clothes from her closet; not forgetting to "borrow" a pair of her cute shoes while I was there.

My daughters are much like Ginni and me, less the fistfights. And like we did, they proclaim that they hate each other occasion-ally. My response is, "Those hormonal emotions will pass with time, girls. Someday you will be best friends." They usually grim-ace, roll their eyes and follow it with a "Sure Mom. What's it like in Utopia" remark. I just grit my teeth and keep in mind that my "precious" daughters believe I am so old, that I had lattes with Noah on the Promenade deck of the biblical Ark, pretty much like Ginni and I did when Grandma gave us the same speech. How I wish I could go back to the day Ginni took me on over that stupid sweater. To me, it would mean more time with her. And I'd still "let her win."

Breast cancer does not run in our family. That was the second reason I didn't react when Ginni told us about the lump she found in her breast. The first reason was ... well, I was a "dork" and didn't take the news seriously. I *could* say that I'm ashamed to admit that I once believed that cancer was a disease that happened to other people, but I'm not. There are some who still think this way and if I can do my part to help those people change their minds, then I will admit to every stupid thought I ever had. Well, *almost* every stupid thought. The rest of them are between God and me, and I sure hope He shows me some mercy when I meet Him face-to-face!

In my early teens as a hospital volunteer, I cared for a few women who were recovering from mastectomies. Not much was known about breast cancer in the 70's. It was believed that it afflicted mostly post-menopausal women. The women I cared for did not seem distraught at all. All of them were over 50. Since I did not detect anguish from those who had just lost their breasts, I assumed this was the only drawback. They sure didn't look bad at all, and they were still spunky enough to bark orders for magazines and chocolates from the gift shop. At my age, the thought of losing my breasts was just a vanity issue. I figured since these women were much older, they were *way* over the "vain thing" anyway. Besides, I had many years of living left before I had to worry myself with *that* stuff, right? I was 13 and "owned the world" so it was easy to understand how I could have bought into the misconception.

In my junior year of high school, I remember a particular day in health class when we passed around a model breast exam teaching aide to help us learn how to do our monthly exams correctly. It resembled a headless and torso less Venus De Milo and it had plastic rubbery skin like Stretch Armstrong. (Ugh, it felt clammy and *gross!)* Our job was to search for the "suspicious lump" in front of our classmates! One could imagine the giggling that went on in that classroom. Well, I was the first to find it. It was near the right armpit area. "Bingo! Do I get a prize?" The teacher did not find any humor in my joke. "Yeah," she said. "You'll get to *live* if you get medical help!" Suddenly, my classmates' attention was off the rubber breasts and on the incredibly ingenious "cut-down" dealt by the teacher. They roared; they pointed, and boy was my face red.

My best friend was concerned about receiving a bad grade on the project, and asked if I could show her where I found the lump. I did. And I offered her my little pearls of wisdom, even though she didn't ask for them. "It felt like a small thread spool to me," I said. "So, I guess cancer feels like a little thread spool or something. I'll know what to search for now. But we don't have to worry about that for a long time, ya know? Only *old* ladies get it." I hope she didn't use those words on the final written exam. She would have flunked it for sure.

In mid October of '86, I was 24 and mother to three-month old Laura. Soon after I had stopped nursing, I developed a large painful lump under my right arm. I didn't do anything about it, thinking it was a side effect from nursing cessation. The lump didn't grow, but it remained painful for more than a month. One sleepless night, I watched "Terms of Endearment" on HBO. Debra Winger's character Emma was diagnosed with cancer soon after her child's pediatrician noticed suspicious lumps under her arm. "Emma" was a young mother with small children, just like me, and she *died* at the end of the movie! (Oops. Sorry about the movie spoiler!) This frightened me so much, I sat at the edge of the sofa right next to the telephone and waited anxiously until 9 a.m. so I could call my doctor. Fortunately, it was only a small infection and it was taken care of immediately.

After my diagnosis, I thought, "What if it *was* cancer? That movie may have well saved my life!" I breathed a big sigh of relief and carried on with life as usual. Within weeks, I had talked myself in to believing once more that breast cancer doesn't happen to younger women, breast cancer feels like a small thread spool, and "Terms of Endearment" is only a movie.

I can't believe what an irresponsible life I lived in the years that followed. Still convinced that breast cancer was an "old lady" disease, I did not do self-breast exams. There was also that dangerous thought tucked way in the back of my mind that what I didn't know couldn't hurt me. If I did not look for lumps, I wouldn't find any. During my annual OB/GYN appointments if the doctor asked if I performed monthly self-exams, I always lied. "Sure! All the time! Sometimes *twice* a month! Everything's good!" Seven years later, Ginni was diagnosed with breast cancer with 7 lymph nodes positive. That could have been me. Only difference is, I would have been dead. Ginni was smart enough to find it and insist that something be done about it.

I'm the older sister and I'm supposed to be the smart one! Well, Ginni was both the cute one and the smart one, leaving me only one of two categories to fall into. No, I'm not the black sheep. (Ginni and I constantly joked about that title rightfully belonging to our brother Wayne.) I was the dreamer and that's pretty obvious in the career paths we pursued. In 1979 at the age of 18, I chose a radio career because all of my life, I've wanted to be in the spot-light. After being a "stay-at-home mom" for most of her married life, Ginni returned to college shortly after being diagnosed with breast cancer and pursued a degree in law. I remember the day she called with her decision. She said, "Life's too short. I'm going to law school."

(College Graduation day! Ginni, far right.)

In 1998 she got herself a "little degree", as she referred to it, and began work as a legal assistant in a family law firm. I was so proud of her, and of course, slightly jealous of her diligence to succeed in such a short amount of time. I often teased her about providing free legal advice to the family. "I'm sorry. I'm for the prosecution," she joked.

I never knew that Ginni's enviable yet sometimes "annoying" qualities would serve as building blocks to the incredible character she possessed in her last 10 years. Not only was she the tomboy, the cute one, and the smart one, she also took what she learned from life to shape her decisions for the future. Some people need a 2 x 4 upside the head; like me, the poster child for denial and procrastination. After Ginni was diagnosed, she provided herself time to "get over herself", and then examined her priorities. Her top priority was to stay alive and raise her children. I'm sure what happened on January 23rd, of 1975 was at the forefront of her mind.

She was 12 and I was 13. Our mother Ruth had been sick for months. She refused to see her doctor because she was afraid that he would admit her into the hospital…again. She couldn't bear the thought of being away from her children for any length of time. Just a couple of years before, Mom had difficulties getting out of bed because of low energy level. She was diagnosed with acute anemia, but doctors could not trace the source. Instead of investigating further, they treated her with high potency iron supplements and transfusions. Sadly, for the anxiety disorder that accompanied her low red count, she was given experimental drugs and electro-shock therapy. Our grandmother (her mother) Estelle took care of us during Mom's hospital stays. Mom occasionally came home most weekends, if she had the energy. Sometimes she would cry because the EST left her with memory gaps. I couldn't understand why Mom was getting worse instead of better. It was after another three month stay she decided that she would never go back…ever.

Grandma had remarried and moved to Arizona with her new husband Henry (whom I call Granddaddy) and our brother Wayne. Our brother Ken lived with Dad, and Ginni, Joannie and I lived with

Mom. Shortly after Grandma moved away, Mom began to show signs of fluid retention around her mid-section. She was always thin and never really ate much. Her skin became discolored and she began to suffer hair loss. She ignored these signs and went about her business as a single mom. Mid October of 1974, she contracted a terrible cold; one that kept her bedridden for weeks on end. She could barely speak and all but stopped eating. Ginni and I begged her to go to the hospital, but she became rather irritated with the both of us for even suggesting it. "They will keep me again," she said. "And this time, I won't come home." Instead, she self-medicated with cough syrup and kept a humidifier running regularly. She swore she would get better.

Granddaddy was in the Army and was just reassigned to Ft. Campbell, KY. On January 20th, 1975, Grandma had persuaded him to bring her to Virginia so she could check on Mom. Her reason why must've sounded absolutely psychotic to Granddaddy, but he readily agreed to leave immediately. Grandma has this scary "gift" that we don't like to speak about. Some believe we have lost league of our senses when we *do* mention it, but Ginni and I knew she had "something." To our knowledge, she was never wrong. Whenever Grandma dreamed of a family member passing away, within days, it happened. Grandma still has this "gift" and I believe Granddaddy is pretty frightened by it himself. Ginni and I always begged her *never* to mention it if she ever dreamed of one of us dying. It was just too creepy.

Mom was upset about the grandparents visit because she didn't want them to know how sick she really was. "I'm fine. It's just the flu," she said. Mom got up for the first time in weeks, put on her best outfit, styled her hair and applied makeup. She acted as if it was another normal day, but I could tell Grandma wasn't buying it. Mom looked frighteningly ill. After I helped her back to bed to "nurse her cold", Grandma told me that she had "one of *those* dreams" again. This time, Mom had died in her sleep. "I just hate them," she sobbed. "God, I hope I'm wrong, but I don't think I am." Mom overheard our conversation and it bothered her. She asked to speak to Grandma privately. Next thing I remember,

Grandma and Granddaddy were leaving. They had only stayed a day, even though they promised us they were staying for the week.

Two days later, around 1 p.m., I went to Mom's room to wake her so she could watch her soaps. She looked as though she was finally sleeping peacefully for the first time in weeks and I was tempted to just let her rest. But I promised, and I didn't want her upset because I didn't do what she asked of me. I tapped her lightly, "Mom? It's 1 o'clock. Time for the soaps." She didn't wake up. I tried again…and again. My voice grew louder. "Mom? Mom? Get up, now. Please Mommy, you're scaring me!" Still nothing. I stared for a moment. She wasn't breathing. I was sure she was dead, and I was frightened to death. We didn't have a phone and the closest pay phone was half a block away. I didn't tell Ginni and Joannie what happened. I just asked Ginni to watch Joannie for a second while I ran out for a second to grab us some lunch. I closed Mom's bedroom door and told the girls not to wake her. I ran out of the house with no shoes on my feet, and headed toward the tiny restaurant on the corner near the main gate of the Shipyard. When I arrived there, I realized I didn't have change for the phone. I fell to my knees and cried. A fireman, who was just finishing his lunch, approached me to question why I was barefoot when there was a measure of snow on the ground. I'm sure it was evident that I was too distraught to care, so he didn't wait for an answer. He offered change to make as many phone calls as I needed. I called the operator first and asked for an ambulance and then called the grandparents. They had just walked in the house from their long trip when they received my call.

The fireman escorted me home. He examined Mom as I explained to my sisters that she was very ill and the ambulance was on the way to take her to the hospital. To my horror, it wasn't an ambulance that arrived. It was a hearse! I asked the fireman why the "spooky-mobile" was sent and he said that all of the ambulances were in route to several car accidents due to the snow. I didn't care. I was so angry that they had the nerve to use the "dead people car" to take Mom to the hospital.

Mom was pronounced dead right where she was. Ginni and Joannie were in her bedroom doorway when her death was confirmed. Joannie refused to speak. It was just two days before her 6th birthday. Ginni was hysterical and screamed as though someone was stabbing her. I knew it was up to me to console her, but I was useless because I couldn't control my own emotions. There were no other family members in the house when this occurred. We were alone and afraid. A longtime friend of the family, John Fridley, volunteered to stay with us until our grandparents arrived. To this day, John is considered a blessed member of our family.

Ginni and I often talked about the events before and after Mom's death. It was the coroner's report that troubled us most. Cause of death was listed as "Cirrhosis of the liver and kidney failure. Alcohol suspected." It didn't make any sense to either one of us. Mom was only 29 years old when she died, and she rarely drank. After sharing this information with medical professionals over the years, we were convinced there was another undiagnosed health issue that was aggravated by the high doses of iron and multitude of experimental medications she was treated with during her lengthy hospital stays. In 1975, most liver damage deaths were probably chalked up to alcohol abuse anyway. Fortunately, medical science has proven that this is not always true. Ginni's own CT scans showed liver scarring which resembled the effects of alcohol; however, years if chemo was the culprit. I'll never know the real reason why Mom died and I cannot change what is written on the death certificate. Given the severity of her symptoms in the year before her death, I do know that's it unlikely that she would have survived had she agreed to go to the hospital when Ginni and I asked her to. And I do know she would have been admitted again, which was against her wishes. Mom created a Last Will and Testament approximately three months prior to her death. I suspect she knew that she didn't have long.

If any good could be seen in this tragedy, it was the experience that helped build the strength Ginni required to take on the battle she would endure as a young woman. I believe God *knew* if He could depend on one person to allow patience, grace and the will to live to radiate through heartbreak, she was the woman for the job.

When God Reached Down His Hand

Time on earth is strictly measured; we're always keeping track
But once it's gone, you can't replace it or ever bring it back
And so we've learned from you, sweet Ginni, to cherish every day
To hug, to love, to treasure each other, before time slips away

Every child is a gift from God, an example of His grace
And sending you to be our angel, made this world a better place
God's call for you to come back home, was hard to understand

But we let go, so you could soar when God reached down His hand
They say that miracles are few these days, but I don't think that's true
For each of us received a miracle when we were touched by you
Just like a graceful butterfly, you've found a place to land
An angel found her wings again when God reached down His hand

© 2005 Merissa Lee Kelley

Today, I am truly blessed by:

Ginni married her high school sweetheart on New Year's Eve 1982. The following year, her husband enlisted in the US Army and a year later, she gave birth to her first child; a son Edward Christopher. Katelyn Elizabeth followed two years later. After living in Germany for over two years, they eventually settled at Ft. Hood, TX where Tyler Jesse later joined his brother and sister.

One afternoon in May of '93, Ginni enjoyed playtime in the family room with Jesse. As she was on her hands and knees, she felt a lump when her right breast rubbed against the inside of her arm. She stopped her activities for a moment to examine it. It was different from any of the other lumps. She immediately made an appointment with her doctor to have it investigated further. Meanwhile, she frightened herself with thoughts of the worst.

Ginni called that afternoon. She was nervous, but I kept assuring her that she was fine. I told her the story of the mass that I found under my arm, and it was only a small infection. "That's probably all it is, Ginni. Don't worry; it's not what you believe it is." Judging by her sighs and sniffles, I don't think she was comforted at all. "Yeah, that's probably all it is," she said softly. "But I gotta be sure, ya know?" I thought she worried about it too much. I figured since she nursed Chris for 15 months and Katy for a year and did not nurse Jesse at all, that was perhaps part of her problem. My first aid kit diagnosis wasn't much different than her family doctor's:

"When I went to the appointment I was asked the usual questions, such as "Do you have any family history of breast cancer?" I had to answer no because I was unaware of any familial links. "Do you take the birth control pill?" No. I tried for 2 weeks once and had reactions. "Have you ever nursed

any of your children?" Yes, I nursed my first two for 15 and 12
months respectively. Well, in answering these questions I was
told that the lump was probably "fibrocystic" because of my
age, no family history, no birth control pills and I nursed my
children. I was told to cut out caffeine and it would get better. I
was relieved and went on with my life of being a young military
spouse, and mother of 3 children."

She called as soon as the appointment was over. She
sounded relieved, "I gotta stop the caffeine" she laughed nervously.
"It's sure gonna be hard to give up that coffee first thing in the
morning!" I laughed with her, "See? I told ya, Dork! Listen to your
older sister for once, will ya? Buy some decaf." There was a
momentary pause, and then she retorted, "Uh .... No, I don't think
so. Decaf is a tease."

Ginni didn't say anything more about the mass in the months
that followed. We moved on with life as normal, running up high
phone bills; chattering about the children, country music, family
gossip and current events. There were no indications that she was
still concerned, so I assumed it was finally over. All of that changed
the following year.

I still carry a burden concerning an incident between Ginni
and me on July 4th of '94. Claus (my husband at the time) and I
customarily took the girls to Avon NC for about a week every
summer. Ginni had taken a spur of the moment trip from Texas to
Newport News to visit the grandparents. The military life had taken
Ginni all over the world so we hadn't seen each other face to face
in years. I really craved that quality time with my sister. I called
Grandma and offered a couple of the rooms in the timeshare and
asked if they would like to enjoy vacation with us. Grandma discussed it with Granddaddy and Ginni and called back to accept the
invitation for a day. I was so excited; I actually used a vacuumed!

(Everyone who knows me can confirm that vacuum cleaners and I don't get along well.) I cleaned up the house (shocking), and went grocery shopping as I anxiously awaited their arrival.

About 5 hours later, they arrived. Ginni greeted my husband and me with a small hello and an embrace. She didn't say much. She looked very unhappy, so I asked her if she felt well. She assured me she was fine, just tired from the trip. Within 15 minutes, she announced that she was going to walk the beach and would return in about 30 minutes. I watched her from the kitchen window. She walked unhurriedly with her head bowed low; as though she were carefully counting her steps. I lost sight of her after a couple of minutes.

When she returned, she asked to speak to the grandparents privately. I left the room but couldn't help to believe that Ginni was angry with me for one reason or another and I couldn't grasp why. Their conversation took less than 5 minutes and I admit I was jealous that I wasn't included on this family "secret." Naturally, I assumed this "secret" was about *me.*

Granddaddy broke the news. "We need to leave after dinner. Your grandmother doesn't like to leave the cat alone overnight." What a lame excuse, I thought. They were leaving because of a stupid cat? By then, I was convinced I had done something to cause "hate and discontent" within the family. Yes, I was *that* insecure. The house was beautiful; it was right on the seaside, there was plenty of food, what else could they need? I didn't understand the "cat" nonsense, so obviously it *had* to be *me.* I laughed. It was more of an irritated laugh than anything. "You're kidding, right? What's the real reason you're leaving?" Same answer. I lost my temper quickly; I didn't even think before I spoke. I started shooting off words that should never be spoken in front of *anybody*, and especially not the parents. Today, I can't believe the things I said, and I sure don't ever want to repeat them. I escorted them all to the door. They said nothing. Within 5 minutes, they were gone.

I cried like a cross between Lucy Ricardo and a sick coyote when they left. Claus showed no mercy and looking back, I can't say I blame him. "You know, you were very rude to them. You need to calm down and call them later when you've got your head screwed on right." I was more than shocked. I was on the verge of screaming at that point, but I had done enough damage. "Obviously you missed what was going on here." He smirked, "Obviously, I didn't." I stormed out of the house, walked to the beach and stayed there till sunset nursing my bruised ego. "What were they hiding from me and why won't Ginni speak to me?"

Over the next four weeks, I avoided phone calls from both Ginni *and* Grandma. Ginni sent a letter, and when I received it, I wrote on the envelope "Return to Sender" and gave it back to the mail carrier. It had been more or less a month since the episode, and I was still behaving like a butthead.

In August, I eventually got over myself enough to call Grandma and attempt to work that whole mess out. It broke my heart when she answered. The first thing out of my mouth was, "I'm sorry." And she cried. She said she hated that I was angry, and she had been upset since it happened. I felt like pond scum. My grandmother cried for weeks and I did not care? I could have kicked myself. "Has Ginni called you?" she asked. I had to tell her the truth. "I avoided her calls and her letter, Grandma. I'll give her a call this evening, maybe we can work this out." What she said next was like a knife in my heart. "She has breast cancer," she said sobbing. It seemed like 10 minutes before I was able to say anything intelligible. And when I did, I was in denial. "No she doesn't! Is it that same lump? The doctors told her it was fibro! What makes her believe she has cancer anyway?" Grandma cried so hard I barely understood what she said next. "She knows she has cancer. She had a biopsy, and it's cancer for sure." Several thoughts came on at once, and I was dizzy from the inner cranial train wreck. They're wrong. Cancer doesn't run in our family. She's too young. I took a deep breath and knew I had to ask the question that had been nagging at me for weeks. "Is this the reason you, Granddaddy and Ginni left the beach house so abruptly?" "Sort of," she said. "Ginni was scheduled for the biopsy

and she was concerned because the lump had grown. She wasn't herself and did not want to spoil your vacation." I sensed myself becoming even more upset. "Why didn't you tell me?" Grandma said, "Ginni didn't want to worry you." I tried to accept that explanation. "So, the cat was really an excuse, huh?"
"No, I don't like to leave Fluffy alone."
"You're kidding me, right? Fluffy is a big girl, she can take care of herself for a day."
"I was worried that she would get into trouble while I was gone," she explained. I couldn't help to chuckle. It was then I remembered the nickname that Ginni and Wayne had for the cat. "Duffy." It was short for "Dumb Fluffy."

If I only knew then what I know now, I wouldn't have been such a prima donna. As I am writing of this incident, I am in the "wait and see" position like she was and I am experiencing the situation from *her* perspective. I cannot believe I only thought of my bruised feelings in her time of need. I understand now why she didn't want to worry us. Unless we had something substantial to be concerned about, fretting while waiting only took precious moments from our lives. She already had to deal with the matter herself; she did not want me to do it as well. She didn't record the temper tantrum incident in her journal. She actually said she had a wonderful time. I'm grateful she omitted that part, but I can't help to believe that this story needed to be shared. If something can be learned of it, it's that we shouldn't let our minds run away with us when we don't understand something. Chances are it's not what we think.

"Love does not hold grudges and will hardly ever notice when others do it wrong. It is never glad about injustice but rejoices whenever truth wins out. If you love someone, you will be loyal to him no matter what the cost. You will always believe in him, always expect the best of him and always stand your ground in defending him."

Thank you for loving me Ginni.

In early 1994 the lump had grown in size and I was get-
ting suspicious but not overly concerned because I had the
"no risk factors" on my side. By now I had moved to Texas
and in a new medical environment; this meant learning the
system all over again. I made an appointment with a family
practitioner and was told the same thing: "fibrocystic breast
disease." I made an appointment with OB/GYN for a pap smear
and this doctor was a little concerned about the lump. He sent
me for a mammogram. The only way to explain the attempted
mammogram experience is to say that I was laughed out of the
department. I was too young for a mammogram, and besides,
only surgeons can order a mammogram for someone of my
age. Well, off I trot back to my GYN doc. Standing in the hall-
way crying, I ask, "Is it possible for a woman of my age to
have breast cancer?" He said simply: "Yes." That was the fuel
I needed. He wrote me a consult for surgery.

Surgery was a new experience. In May of 1994 I met with
a surgeon who told me, "If you are worried about breast can-
cer, I can take them both off." Imagine my shock at that state-
ment! He did however order a mammogram. By this time, my
lump had developed an internal itch. Of course, this was not

supposed to be a sign of breast cancer. "Cancer does not itch," I was told. I had the mammogram done, and while the lump did not show up, it could be felt and had grown considerably since I first discovered it. The mammography report suggested a follow-up since there existed something of an asymmetry between the left and right breasts. I was getting ready to go on vacation for a month, and the surgeon was leaving for some military deployment, so between us, we agreed that if the lump and itch had not resolved themselves by August, he would perform a biopsy.

I went on vacation to my home state of Virginia. Looking back, it was a wonderful time. I felt good. I didn't feel sick and enjoyed immensely the time spent with my family and friends. All the time, however, the lump was growing, the itch increasing and now the skin was red where the lump was. I remember laying on the beach one day and feeling shock at how the lump had changed but still had some comfort in that the doctors must know what they were talking about. They see cancer everyday; they certainly would know if mine was cancer.

In August, 1994, I went in for the biopsy. The surgeon told me all the way into the OR that he was certain it was not cancer because it did not "feel" like cancer. During the biopsy I roused a little and felt the surgeon tugging. I started to cry. He placed his hand on my head and I went back to sleep. I woke up in a private room. Starved silly the nurse brought me lunch and I jumped into the sandwich happily because the biopsy was over and no one had said anything to me about it being cancer. My surgeon walked into the room then and stood at the foot of the bed. He said, "It's malignant" I looked at him for a moment trying to recall, "Is malignant the bad one or good one?" It then dawned on me what he had said. He immediately launched into how he had set me up for surgery the following week, and how we needed to start chemotherapy, and on and on... I called him a liar and threw my sandwich at him. He didn't flinch but I noticed tears in his eyes. Here was *the doctor who had told me if I was worried about breast cancer; he would take them both off, with tears in his eyes.*

I simply can't imagine her being looked at as a "hypochondriac" in the mammogram department. This breaks my heart, however, that was 1994. I am grateful that she didn't take the original diagnosis as gospel; otherwise we wouldn't have had the extra years with her.

That moment started me down a path from which there is no road back. I chose a modified radical mastectomy because at the moment of diagnosis I wanted the cancer off of me. It felt as though I was dirty and the only way to get clean was to get the cancer far away from me. Once the mastectomy was done, my prognosis came in. All the tests were done to determine where I stood as a cancer patient. The lump was identified as infiltrating ductal carcinoma. The size was 7.5 cm. I had 6 positive lymph nodes. The tumor was positive for estrogen and progesterone receptors. My S-phase was 5%. What does all that mean? How it was explained to me was that I had a very large tumor that had spread to the lymph nodes but if I was going to get cancer it was the kind I wanted. (?) Your garden variety cancer it was said. The hormone receptors were good because that meant I could benefit from the new drug Tamoxifen. The S-Phase meant the tumor cells divided slowly and I did not have an aggressive tumor. Basically, I was sick but they could save me.

I immediately had a port put in so that I could receive chemo through it. In removing lymph nodes the surgeon took over 30 so my right arm could no longer have any blood pressure or needle sticks in it due to the lack of lymph nodes to fight off any infections. This left only the left arm accessible for needle sticks. The port was a great option for me at the time. On 16 September 1994 I started chemo: Adriamyacin, Cytoxan, and 5FU. Six cycles every twenty-one days. The oncologist told me he wanted to treat me aggressively with as high a dosage of the chemo as I could tolerate without killing me. Basically I felt I was risking my life just to save it.

I still entertained wishful thinking that she was misdiagnosed, but I had to learn to accept that my sister had cancer. I had no reassuring words for. I used what I had when I tried to reassure her that she was not sick. My next job would be more difficult; trying to convince her and myself that she was not going to die.

"The cancer may get me, but it's going to have to catch me first!" I'm off on a new road God is leading me down. God, give me the grace to make it moment by moment.

Today, I am truly blessed by:

"I have asked the question a time or two about 'why me?' "Why do I have cancer?" I think we all ask a similar question in our life. It's an awesome thought for me to know that God has looked at the cancer long before I ever got it and has approved me for it. I believe I can handle it if He has surveyed and put his stamp of approval on it."

At first, Ginni updated us with details that we wanted to hear. I learned quickly that Ginni, at times, was much like our grandmother when it came to discussing her health. Grandma never wanted to worry anyone, so she would either say she was fine or give us as little information as possible. I hated that. Fortunately, Ginni realized that hiding her condition wasn't fair to those who loved her. After 5 years, she finally revealed the severity of her illness.

She planned a sibling's night out in November 1999. Ginni, Wayne, Joannie and I stopped into a little beer joint called "The Ponderosa" on Jefferson Avenue, Newport News. It had been there for so many years the clientele never changed. It was an old establishment, reminiscent of a typical 1960's watering hole with a live band playing old Merle Haggard and George Jones tunes. Rum and cokes were cheap and it wasn't nearly as crowded as the larger nightclubs. We spent most of the evening joking around with one another. Ginni and Joannie told almost every male in the club that I was unloved and needed someone to dance with. I hate to dance, but they tried their best to get me to "lighten up." They did whatever it took. I was asked to dance at least 30 times, and each time I respectfully declined. Ginni whined, "Awww, what if that poor man's life sucks? You could have made his night if you would have just danced with him one stinkin' time, ya dork." I roared, "Ginni, you made me out to be the charity case. They were just trying to help a lonely lady feel loved. Now, shaddap!"

It was almost midnight and my sides hurt from the laughter. All the sudden, Ginni became solemn. "We had fun tonight, but there's a reason I asked for us to get together this evening." I didn't like the sound of this. However, I assumed that it had something to do with her marriage. There wasn't anything going on that I knew of, but I assumed it didn't have anything to do with the cancer because there hadn't been any bad reports. Besides, I had my fill of the cancer scare. I was ready for us to go back to normal and have some more fun. She had tears in her eyes, "The cancer is always going to be there, you know? I'm stable now, but I still have it." Joannie started to cry and stood up from her chair slightly as though she were leaving, but sat back down when Ginni continued, "I will someday die of breast cancer. I hope it's not for a long time, but I sensed I needed to tell you so you won't think I'm keeping anything from you again. I definitely want you to be prepared." All four of us wept silently. I wanted to know more. "Ginni, has the doctor said anything about your condition recently?" She dried her tears and looked me in the eyes, "My condition remains unchanged and so far that's good. But I'm not cancer free and I never will be." My brother breathed a sigh of relief, "So, everything's good for right now, right?" Joannie excused herself to the ladies room, still in tears. Ginni nodded, "Yes, so far everything's fine." I chimed in, "So there's still hope, right?" Ginni smiled, "There's always hope. I'm just saying we need to cherish every moment we have."

"I've heard that the mind and the heart both have individual memories. I've learned it's the heart memories that tug at and free the spirit of life and living. I am a thirty-seven-year old military wife, mother to three precious children, and a six-year survivor of breast cancer. I've lived a cranium full of the typical memories of births, deaths, graduations, moves and equal milestones. Recently I have been diagnosed with early metastasis to the bone. Strangely I am learning something with this diagnosis that I didn't quite grasp the first go round on this ride named cancer---that each and every second of life is so very, very, endearingly special. The smile, the touch, the words, the smells of some of the most everyday of things construct fiercely tender heart memories: the sideways glance of a chastised child; the challenging yet wobbled stance of

teenage independence; a tiny hand wiping a tear over the lost ball game; a smudge of jelly, again, on the cabinet; the smell of a wet dog and little boy; a plea for help with homework; the incessant ringing of a telephone with the sound of clamoring feet to answer it; a yawn and tossled hair at breakfast; and the whispered giggles that fall with the night. Each and every second is a new spirit lifting memory to the heart and a second worth celebrating."

That night, Ginni begged us to live each day to the fullest and to never take anything or anyone for granted. We dried our tears and attempted to go for that laugh again. Wayne asked us to go to an "after hours" club so they could try to get me on the dance floor again; because obviously, I wasn't living life to the fullest! And so we went. I still did not dance, but I did make an effort to "enjoy life"…for her.

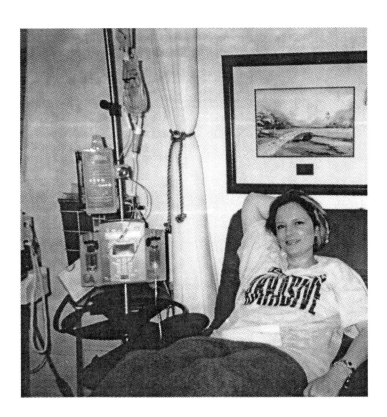

Left to right: Ya-Ya Acinom, Karen and Ginni

Ginni (left) and Ya-Ya CanDSam ham it up in Vegas.

Thank you for the fabulous Ya-Ya Sisterhood, Rebecca Wells!

Ginni often said that she had met so many wonderful people, whom she believed she would not have met if she'd not had breast cancer. She made a connection with someone practically everywhere she went. Grocery store, library, restaurants, you name it. She was never a "wig" person and didn't try to conceal the fact that she had cancer. When people would ask her about her condition, she openly spoke about it, hoping to instill enough information to educate them on how to catch cancer early. She collected phone numbers and email addresses, so when she had the energy, she could follow up on her newfound friends.

Thanks to a book by written by Rebecca Wells*, she became close to a whole group of new friends worldwide!

"...even if you don't have a sister in your life, I urge you to see the movie The Divine Secrets of the Ya-Ya Sisterhood. My wonderful sister took me to see it while I was in Virginia. I also attended one of the local gatherings while there and that began my journey with meeting the most incredible group of women I've ever come across in my life. With contact through the internet site (www.ya-ya.com) I just recently went to my second gathering here in the state of Texas. This one I took my daughter to and it was just as moving as the first gathering. I've met women who truly define the spirit of sisterhood. Women who will tell me to get over myself when I get too whiney and self absorbed and women who will hug me without me even saying I need a hug. I cannot say that I have gone a day without receiving a smile from any number of the wonderful Ya-Ya sisters and for that I am truly blessed and thankful. Thank you, Ya-Yas!"

One of the best things I believe I ever did for her was to introduce her to the "Ya-Ya Sisterhood." We had read the books and loved them, but were compelled to see the movie when we learned that Sandra Bullock would be portraying "Siddalee". It was perfect that afternoon in mid-June of 2002. We went to the Hampton AMC 24 to catch the afternoon matinee of "The Divine Secrets of the Ya-

Ya Sisterhood." We truly loved it and talked about it all the way home. We vowed to find girlfriends just like "Vivi", "Necie", "Caro", and "Teensy".

After Ginni returned to her home in Texas later that week, I searched the Internet to see if there really was such a thing as the "Ya-Ya Sisterhood." I "Googled" Rebecca Wells and found Gumbo Ya-Ya, a message board for Internet sisterhood, moderated by Brenda Stacey, the Ya-Ya Web Hostess. I lurked for a bit and read a few posts before I registered in July 2002 as "royal grand poobah of dust bunnies." (Named for my allergy to vacuum cleaners.) Today, I'm just known as "Poobah", since Gin actually "caught" me vacuuming one afternoon. (It wasn't plugged in. That's my story and I'm sticking to it.)

There was one particular member that I became fond of immediately. She posted much like me and had shared interesting anecdotes about her step-son that I found absolutely hilarious. Mainly because whatever antics she posted seemed to be happening in my own household. It was like she was looking over my shoulder! Her online name was "Trooper." I didn't know what a *trooper* she really was until I started reading more of her posts. She had cancer. Her doctor sent her home to basically "get her affairs in order." I wish I could remember what the whole story was, but what I *did* understand was unacceptable. Trooper was in Houston TX, which was not too far of a drive for Ginni if she needed her. I called Ginni and directed her to the site and the post in particular. That was the day Ginni formally joined Gumbo Ya-Ya as "Trace." And one of her first posts was support for Trooper and an open invitation if she needed someone to talk to. They fast became online friends. Sadly, Trooper passed away less than a year later, truly a sad day on Gumbo.

Ginni continued to post her treatment updates, referring to one of her recurring threads as "Taxotere Tuesday"; named for the brand of chemo she was receiving at the time.

From Gumbo Ya-Ya:

It's hard not to attribute feelings of being unwell to a major illness. I mean, even now when I feel puny, is it because of chemo or side effects of the ten tons of drugs or depression? That's really hard to unwind. Do you keep a journal? Sometimes keeping a journal of how you are feeling might pinpoint what is causing the problem. I think it's funny when I go to a new doc and when they take my vitals and such and are made aware of the cancer, invariably the nurse always asks, 'do you have any other medical conditions?'. My response is, 'isn't cancer enough?' But I understand what she means. I am more than my cancer and can and probably do have other medical conditions. I mean, I AM getting older. I am feeling ok today after Tuesday's treatment. I slept most of Tuesday afternoon and yesterday. If I wasn't sleeping, I was on here. My hair is coming out more but perhaps it won't come out all the way. If it does then I'm prepared with hats and scarves thanks to the Ya-Yas.
I'm going into my make believe job today. I think I feel well enough. May you all have a wonderful day!

She always signed her posts with:

Hugz, Trace

Late January of 2003, there were no "Taxotere Tuesday" updates and the Ya-Yas became concerned. I received calls and emails from the "sisters" inquiring about Ginni's condition. But it wasn't illness that was keeping her away from the sisterhood. Her computer had crashed and she was waiting for one of her friends repair it for her. The "wait" became too long for the Ya-Yas. On the last day of February, the Texas Ya-Yas paid her a surprise visit and delivered a brand new computer!

The plan was the brainchild of one of our longtime Ya-Yas, Laura, better known as "Duchess Singing Moon". At the same time, she was planning another surprise for one of our Canadian Ya-Yas known as Goddess of Giddiness. Goddess of Giddiness was also battling cancer and unable to stay in contact with the online sisters she had grown to love over the years. "Sisters" from all over the world contributed funds for the two computers. February 28th was an exciting day on Gumbo Ya-Ya. We all couldn't wait to read those words: "The Eagle Has Landed!"

Gumbo Ya-Ya "Necie-Cakes" observes Ginni's reaction
"Dude! You got a Dell!"

"What a wonderful day that was. Looking back all I could think of was that I was speechless....boy, when you are in awe, the words don't come easy. But the love sure does from Ya-Ya."

Dixie Doolittle, The Belle From Texas, and Ginni set up the new computer!

Christening the new computer on Gumbo Ya-Ya!

- Rebecca Wells: An American actress, playwright and author. She is best known for her **Ya-Ya** series of novels, published by HarperCollins.

- Gumbo Ya-Ya: Message board linked to Rebecca Wells' website.

Today I am truly blessed by:

"I've gone through many emotional painful trials since the last update and I have to believe that the trials will make me a better person when all is said and done. I do not feel like a better person when I am wallowing in my own pity and despair, how-ever somehow the sun always comes out again and I look back and see how far I've come. It's then that I realize that now is not the time to give up. Now is the time to press on."

Cancer not only hurts the body, it can also destroy relation-ships. It's not fair, but it happens. Sadly, Ginni's marriage ended in divorce in July of 2003. She took 50 percent of the responsibility. She said, "It takes two people to make a marriage and it takes two to end one." I agree with this. However, she was still devastated. She often voiced "what if" musings. This was purely understand-able. After all, they were married for 20 years and had three children together. Nevertheless, the family has accepted the blessing through this turmoil; that she was able to spend her re-maining years with us. When it was time to bring her home, I was more than ready to go to Texas to pick her up, no matter what it took.

I thank God daily for my husband Jim and his best friend Tony. They were so very understanding of my concern and as-sisted me in moving Ginni back to Newport News. She had chil-dren, dog, and years of memories in tow. I know it had to be hard enough to leave everything she loved in Texas behind without having to worry about how she was going to move too. I really wondered how she was going to manage to "stay in today" with another heartbreak added to her list. Tony drove his car and Jim and I drove "The Beast"; a 1998 Chevy Suburban that lived up to it's name gas-wise, but was a comfortable ride nonetheless.

The Texas Ya-Yas held a going away party for Ginni at the home of one of our beloved "sisters" Dixie Doolittle." It was bitter-sweet. Ginni had met so many of them and grown to love them as her own family. Leaving them behind broke her heart, but she knew that miles never kept the Ya-Yas away. They were always either a phone call away, or on the doorstep when she needed them.

Ginni found a rental home in Newport News, and took in an old high school friend as a roommate to help make ends meet. Her oldest son Chris was grown and enlisted in the Army. She continued to raise Katy and Jesse. Aunt Joan, Granddaddy and I took turns taking her to weekly chemo treatments. Ginni was on the road to having everything she needed for survival, but soon, she began missing the fellowship she had in her home church. She was determined to find a new one in Newport News.

One Wednesday night, she and I commenced searching for a church that served a meal before bible study. That night, we had obviously missed "supper" hour when we walked into a bible study at Temple Baptist Church on Harpersville Road. I remember the first reaction. Everyone stopped listening to the Pastor and watched our every move. Yes, we were strangers and we felt a little dopey justly barging into a meeting already in progress, but we're glad we did it. The people we met in that church helped our family enormously through Ginni's ordeal.

Pastor Dave was an incredible speaker. It was the first time in years I had been able to sit through a sermon without nearly dozing off! Barb Spencer, a female deacon, was "assigned" to Ginni and me and we became friends almost immediately. Barb is soft spoken, slow to anger and genuinely compassionate. When Ginni or I required anything or someone to talk us through bad moments, she was there with no questions asked. I believe every woman should have a "Barb" in her life. On so many occasions, she has helped me keep my brain intact when I've felt like calling it quits. My first day back at work after Gin's funeral, Barb called and said she felt a burden for me and called to see if I was okay. Just seconds before, I had cried out to God to help me get through that day. Barb was an immediate answer to prayer. Sometimes I wonder, "Who is Barb's 'Barb'? Barb needs a 'Barb'! Everyone…and I mean *everyone* should have a "Barb."

We continued to attend Temple Baptist. Ginni went most every Sunday and Wednesday when she wasn't suffering side effects of chemo. I went with her when I wasn't working. I appreciated the time, not just for bible study and fellowship, but quality time with Ginni. We often planned our after-church activities by writing notes to each other on the back of the church bulletin:
"Wanna do lunch and Wal-Mart? I need new lipstick."
"Sure! You pick the restaurant and it's your turn to pay."
Most of the time, we didn't make it home till dark. My husband got used to being alone on Sundays and usually prepared his own plans for the day. Hanging out with two giggling sisters on a shopping spree wasn't his idea of a good time.

I remember one Sunday while driving home from Wal-Mart, Ginni began thinking about her marriage, and started to cry. It broke my heart to see her like that. She begged me to help her take her mind off it. After I stopped at a red light, I reached over and kissed her on the cheek and dried her tears. At first, I didn't see the red truck in the other lane also stopped at the light. It was after I kissed her that I glanced at the man in the red truck. He was bouncing in his seat, smiling from ear to ear; giving us the "two thumbs up." I said to Ginni, "Look at that man next to us, will ya?" The look on her face was priceless. Wide eyes filled with amusement, mouth agape. "He thinks we're gay!" She roared. "What a blessing! That man just helped me out of my funk! How funny is that?" It was amazing how she managed to see a blessing in that situation, but it didn't surprise me. "Blessings are everywhere," she often said. "You just have to expect them, and be constantly on the lookout for them." I still smile when I think of this man, out there somewhere; clueless that he single-handedly turned my sister's tears into laughter.

"So if I pray for God to heal me, it may not be his will. And if it's not, then 2 Corinthians 12:9 says that His "strength is made perfect in weakness." So, I feel that if God chooses not to heal me, then He has a plan down the road for me so that he can be glorified through my weakness. I am going to learn something more through this and it's not clear yet. Again, one day at a time needs to be taken."

Ginni's oncologist gave her more disturbing news soon after we returned from a Ya-Ya gathering in Las Vegas in September 2003. Her condition remained stable, though her tumor markers continued to rise. She was switched from Taxotere to Navelbine, and kept plugging along, even though she was disappointed that the name "Navelbine Tuesday" didn't carry that same poetic "ring" on Gumbo Ya-Ya. The doctor said as long as the cancer, which had metastasized to bone, did not affect soft tissue, she could remain in stable condition indefinitely. Scans were done monthly to make sure that this didn't happen, although we had quite a scare when suspicious "spots" were detected on her lungs and liver. The doctor wasn't sure if they were cancerous, but continued to keep an eye out for changes. Meanwhile, her chemo was switched again; this time to Gemzar. When one chemo would stop working, Ginni always asked the doctor, "What else is in your back pocket?" Then, she and her oncologist would make their game plan.

Some treatments wreaked havoc on Ginni's bones. Both of her ankles became brittle and eventually broke while she was washing dishes one evening. Her doctor ordered surgery immediately to implant pins in the weak areas. This worried her because she knew after surgery she would need 24-hour care. Rich and Lisa Evans, a young couple from Temple Baptist, took Ginni and the children in for the weeks she needed to recover. I offered, but Ginni knew I would be working most days. Rich and Lisa gave her and the children their own rooms, and they cared for her everyday for six weeks. I usually dropped by after work so we could watch court shows and "Reba", and enjoy a few games of Yahtzee. (And she usually won, claiming she was the 'Yahtzee Champeeeeen of the WORLD!') I don't know if Rich and Lisa really know how deeply the family appreciates what they did for our precious Ginni, but I know for sure they absolutely adored her as though she were a member of their *own* family.

October 20th, 2004, I had breast surgery of my own. I had a benign lump removed and a reduction. When I woke up from my anesthesia induced stupor, I saw Ginni within inches of my face. "How are you feeling? Are you in pain? Do you need a pillow? Is your stomach upset?" I don't remember how I answered because I was somewhat out of it, but I do remember my throat was extremely sore. And I remember Ginni pretending to be an emergency room doctor screaming, "She needs Phenergan in her IV, STAT!" I thought, "Why am I paying these doctors and nurses? Ms. Monk needs to be on the payroll!"

During my recovery at home, Ginni stayed in my bed right next to me, constantly reminding me to take my medication on time so I could "stay ahead of the pain." With all she had been through, she knew all about pain management. Besides, even though Ginni was a good soul, she would nag me to death if I didn't take my medication as directed. She made me wonder why she chose law over a medical career.

I remained at home for over a week after the surgery. Ginni called one afternoon while I was sleeping off some pain meds. "How do you feel?" she asked. "Groggy and achy." I replied. "Hey! I need you to stay well. The doctor wants to get me into the allogenic stem cell trial at NIH." I paused for a moment. I don't think it had really sunk in. "Um…allogenic stem cell? NIH?" I moaned. "Yes, a stem cell transplant from a sibling. It's a clinical trial being conducted at National Institutes of Health in Bethesda." It sounded promising to me, but I was also concerned. Was she getting sicker? "Ginni, you know I'll do it. Just tell me where to sign up. But leave me 'lone now. I'm tired." She laughed, "Yeah, in a minute. Anyway, I'll need a stem cell transplant from a matching brother or sister, you know. And if any of you are, that will totally wreck my claims of being adopted." I could have smacked her. I was still in pain and she continued to make me laugh. After I hung up, I thought about the prospect, and in my gut, I knew I was her stem cell match. I can't explain it, but it was like God talking to my soul. Not audibly. It was something in my knower.

Mid January 2005, Ginni called at 6 a.m. *just* as I was slapping the snooze button for the fourth time. She had a dream that she wanted to share with me and it couldn't wait. "What is it?" I asked. "I dreamed that you were my stem cell match. Is it just wishful thinking or do you think it's a sign?" I knew it had to be a sign. There was just no other explanation. God was doing so many miraculous things in our lives. I told her what my heart was saying since the day she asked me to "stay well."

Within the week, Wayne, Ken, Joannie and I were tested for compatibility. On February 8th, 2005, Ginni called just as I was finishing my show. "Are you sitting down?" she asked. "Do I need to?" I joked. "You're the match!" John Shomby, my boss, could hear my screams all the way down the hallway. "I'm a match! I'm a match!" I cannot ever recall being that excited my entire life!

I truly feel that God blessed me with John Shomby as my boss, but more importantly as my friend. I believe John was sent to work at The Eagle in *His* perfect time. When I talked with him about taking the time off to go through with this procedure, frankly I was worried. However, I worried for nothing. John was genuinely compassionate and understanding. I learned quickly that John is one who puts family first and encourages us to do so as well. He followed Ginni's progress since he arrived at The Eagle and offered his prayers for her recovery. It was as though he loved her from day one. I remember the first time John "met" Ginni. I should have warned him that she would latch on to his heart instantly. Anyway, Ginni had been hounding me for weeks to come to Texas for a gathering of the Ya-Yas at a ranch in Round Top. I told her that we were very busy around that time and I didn't think John could spare me. Actually, I was too chicken to ask him but I didn't tell *her* that. Ginni was persistent. She rarely took "no" for an answer. She made her final plea when she *knew* I was in one of my weekly meetings with John. She called my cell phone and asked to speak with him, and I reluctantly let her, believing I knew where it was going. When John told her that he would allow me to take a couple of days, she screamed so loud, he had to pull the phone away from his ear. He chuckled, "She ain't excited, is she?" It was such a cute moment. I wonder if he knew how much she adored him from that moment on?

Almost daily, John would ask about Ginni's progress. Some people do that for idle chit-chat, but I could tell he really wanted to know. So when it was time to ask for vacation and sick days for the procedures, I had barely opened my mouth before John said, "Go!

Your job is always here. Take care of Ginni." He walked me through all of the paperwork and I was on my way before I knew it. The church and the Ya-Yas stepped up to the plate and took care of our families while we were away. This was all such a blessing that came on so fast, it was hard *not* to see God's hand in it all.

Ginni and her beloved "Arf Flea Bailey." Bailey passed away peacefully September 2006 after a short battle with thyroid cancer.

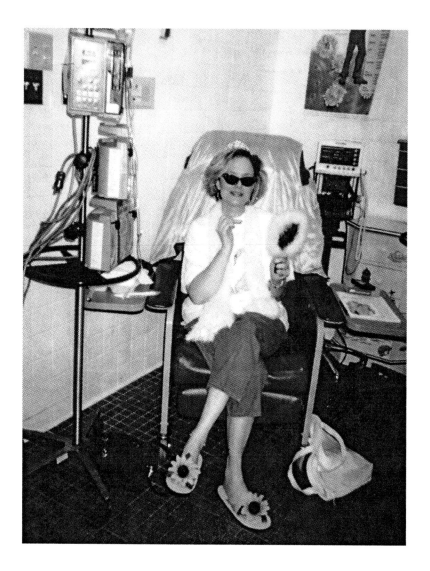

"Everyone should have a tiara, boa, and cute shoes for chemo day!"

Today, I am truly blessed by:

In February, we went to NIH in Bethesda for extensive testing. My testing took one day...Ginni's took 4. They checked us for everything from HIV to West Nile to infections in the toenails. We were checked from top to bottom, asked embarrassing questions, and poked and prodded. That's okay. After all, we were Ya-Yas, so we "glammed" it up during each procedure; tiaras, boas and all. After that, we were sent home to rest so we could return in early March to get the ball rolling.

February 26th, we were paid a surprise visit from three of our Ya-Ya sisters! Lisa (a.k.a. Princess Kicking Bear), Linda (a.k.a. Cross-stitch Ya-Ya), and Stormy. They brought all the fixin's for a big weekend "pre-transplant" pajama party! The house was flowing with chocolate, pizza, pasta prepared by Linda, and tons of laughter. It was exactly what the "doctor ordered", as far as I'm concerned. Neither Ginni nor I posted our apprehensions the upcoming adventure, but the girls knew we needed "something", and came bearing gifts of comfort. Lisa said the "theme" of the gifts was "things that are soft", like warm socks, lotions, soothing music CDs and inspirational books. Lisa made soft blankets with bears and bunnies for each of us, and Ginni and I adored them. They were going to be perfect to snuggle up with while we had our procedures.

Ginni, Lisa (a.k.a. Princess Kicking Bear) & Karen

"The clinical trial officially begins. My prayer is that if it's God's will, I will receive supernatural healing and God will be glorified in this trial."

Ginni began pre-transplant chemo on March 2nd. March 3rd, I spent 3 hours on the apheresis giving lymphocytes; cells to be used to inject Ginni after the transplant to help her avoid contracting Graph VS Host disease; an immune attack on the recipient by cells from a donor. The apheresis is a large machine that separates stem cells, lymphocytes and plasma from other cells. Tubes are placed in the left arm where the blood is extracted and processed through the machine. The blood is returned to the body through another tube inserted in the right arm or hand.

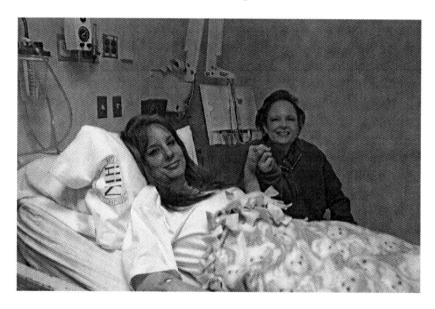

Between March 3rd and the 7th, I had to inject myself twice daily with Neupogen; a drug to stimulate the stem cells. I thought I only had to inject once a day, but our cutie Research Nurse Michael called while I was hanging around with Ginni during chemo. "I'm sorry," he said. "We'll need you to inject yourself twice a day. I hope this is not an inconvenience for you. I owe you lunch." It was for Ginni, so nothing was an inconvenience as far as I was concerned. Besides, Nurse Michael could have asked Ginni or me to cluck like a chicken in the middle of the beltway and we would have considered it. He was just adorable! Sadly, I'm still waiting on that lunch.

Ginni laughed watching me self inject. I mean, she was an old pro, and I looked like a 3 year old crying over a broken toy! She joked that she hoped I would draw blood. She said she had done it so many times, she'd think she was cursed if I hadn't done it at least once. She got her wish. On the last injection before the second apheresis procedure, I was so excited to finally be finished with those injections, that I poked myself too fast. Not only did I draw blood, I left a nice little bruise on my upper right thigh. Oh well, I laughed with her, even though it smarted like the dickens.

On March 7 at 7 a.m., it was time to give the actual stem cells. By then, the Neupogen had made me so sick; I didn't care what the nurse did to me. She could have robbed me blind, fed me calves liver, and pelted me with acorns and I would have just laid there and whined. I was given Emla to numb both arms. Nurse Gail (pictured) hooked me up and I lay still for 6 hours while the apheresis did its job. Danged machine looked and sounded like a washing machine! The actual donation part didn't hurt so terribly! As a matter of fact, the more stem cells they took from me, the better I felt. Nurse Gail, Ginni and I watched movies and ate jelly bellies during the process. I thought I was going to have to stop before the 6 hours was up, though. I was given at least 4 liters of fluid during the procedure and was having a difficult time with the whole bedpan notion. (You can't get out of the bed during the entire 6 hour stretch.) Fortunately, I completed the cycle. I couldn't wait for Nurse Gail to take the IVs out. My eyes were floating out of my skull by then. I asked her to cut the tubes off instead of removing them and let me hit the potty. I figured I'd have blessed relief a lot faster that way. Ginni said I looked like an antelope when I hopped out of the bed and dashed to the ladies room. I heard her laughing. I yelled out, "Not funny, sis! I owe you! You are drinking a gallon of tea before bedtime, Missy! Got it?"

Doctors needed 3 million stem cells in order to have a successful transplant. If they didn't get at least 3 million, I would have to repeat the procedure the following day. That evening, we received a call with the news. Ginni couldn't wait to record it in her journal.

"My sister gave up her stem cells today. What a trooper! She lay in the bed with her right arm strapped down and her left arm minimally strapped for 6 hours. She did so much better than I ever would. The last hour, she had to go potty and had issues with the bedpan. I tried to take her mind off of it, but she watched the clock. She made it, though. They wanted her to give at least 3 million stem cells. She gave 11 million! AMEN!"

That was Ginni's last entry.

Meanwhile, she was instructed to stay away from people who were ill, and I was asked to bring her back to NIH in two weeks to prepare for the transplant. On March 23rd, we returned and I admitted Ginni. I knew I was going to cry when I left her. Fortunately, my friend and Ya-Ya sister Stormy drove up from Charlottesville to accompany me home. I made plans to return to NIH that weekend with a care package of magazines, chocolate, and clean clothes.

The following day, I went to my grandparent's home to visit with my Aunt Gerry and Cousins Janice and Karen who were in town from Buena Vista, VA for the day. Grandma prepared a celebration lunch complete with a huge Smithfield ham. Aunt Joan was there too. (Ginni always said, where ever there was ham, there was Aunt Joan.) We sat down together to thank God for the miracle that was to come with the stem cell transplant. We gathered around the table and held hands to pray for Ginni's recovery. We conversed about having Ginni with us after the 100 critical days in the hospital, and planned another celebration around it. It was a warm and powerful feeling being among family, but it still felt strange not having her there with us.

Midway through lunch, I received a call on my cell phone. The area code was Maryland and I assumed it was Ginni calling to chat a bit before her surgery to insert a new port for transplant use. It wasn't. It was one of the doctors from the transplant team. "Is this Ms. Michek's sister?" I knew it couldn't be good. "Yes," I said. "Is she okay?" Obviously, she wasn't. The doctors on the transplant team believed that her pain medications were backing up in her liver. They also said that the last two scans had shown that the cancer had become aggressive in the liver area, and created a blockage. "Is she okay?" I asked again. "We're going to need you to come back here as soon as possible. We're not going to be able to do the transplant." The tears started flowing before she got the last word out. I couldn't believe it. She was fine when I left her and now all of the sudden, they don't want to go through with the transplant? It could not be happening. "Why can't you?" I screamed. "We'll discuss this all together when you arrive. When do you think you'll be here?" I looked at my husband Jim and said, "We have to go back. Can we leave now?" He agreed. "I'm on my way. I'll be there in about 4 to 5 hours." We said goodbye. Everyone at the table remained quiet except for my grandmother. "What is happening?" She had tears streaming down her face already. "I don't know the whole story, Grandma. The doctor said that they won't be able to do the transplant. She said something about not being able to wake Ginni up this morning! I don't understand it. I hope she wasn't trying to tell me that Ginni took a turn for the worst. I need to get back up there and put my foot down or something. We haven't gotten this far for nothing." Aunt Joan kept saying, "Go! Go!" as I was getting my things together. I called John Shomby to alert him that I was on my way back to NIH because something had gone wrong. I called Ginni's son Christopher and he made the trip with my husband and me.

I spoke with every doctor on Ginni's transplant team after we were told there was nothing more they could do for her. NIH had already called hospice in Newport News. They said that giving her the transplant at this stage in her disease would only kill her sooner. My heart was broken. I took a deep breath to try to calm the electric shock sensations I was feeling in my chest. I couldn't accept that she didn't have but days or maybe weeks to live. To my knowledge, when I admitted her for transplant, she was in stable condition. Ginni, Chris and I begged the doctors to do the transplant anyway. What did we have to lose? But they refused. It was explained that she would die immediately if she went through with it. Taking her home would give her a chance to "get her affairs in order."

I refused to take her home until another series of blood tests was performed, so we stayed for another few days. I continued to beg her transplant team not to give up. I must have sounded like a broken record, but I wasn't going to stop even if I was forced to. I know Ginni wouldn't have given up on me if the situation were reversed. We loved each other that much! Chris even volunteered part of his liver. He begged just as much as I did.

I called my "Barb" and asked her to put the church on alert. We needed more prayer. Not only did she get the word out, she picked up Katy and Jesse and a cooler of food and drove immediately to NIH. She held our hands and prayed with us. She encouraged us to stay positive and seek the Lord's face. After the visit, she took the children out to dinner, and drove them back to Newport News. She continued to call several times a day for updates. Nothing had changed on March 27th. Her bilirubin level kept rising;

an indication that her liver was failing. Ginni and I agreed to go home, but we didn't plan to give up the fight.

She asked me to make sure to tell the family what was going on with her and to assure them that we would continue to pray for a miracle. I agreed. I asked her what she wanted me to say to the Ya-Yas. She said, "The truth." That night before we checked out, I posted this on Gumbo Ya-Ya:

About Trace:

This is so hard for me to post…but I knew I was the one who had to do it. I waited a few days to tell you because I had to make sure the family knew first.

Trace and I are going home tonight. The cancer in her liver is aggressive and to do the transplant would kill her. Doctors felt it was in her best interest to go home and be with family. Believe me, I've had the doctors run and rerun the tests several times and they were more than willing to do that…but nothing has changed.
I asked Trace how I should tell you…and she said just to tell you the truth. We don't know how much time is left. It could be a few days, weeks or maybe a month or two.

I am meeting with the hospice nurse and our pastor tomorrow. This is definitely the hardest thing I've ever been through in my life. This girl is my best friend…I love her more than I love myself. I feel like I am losing a part of me.

Doctors have agreed to continue taking blood tests with her on-cologist back home. Her bilirubin level is high. It has remained at the same level for 4 or 5 days. It hasn't gone up any nor has it gone down. That level would have to go down significantly in order for her to be considered for the transplant again…but doctors don't believe it's going to happen because the disease has taken control of the liver. There's still always that small hope for a miracle…and we never give that up.

If it's God's time for her to go home, then she and I both know where she is going and we're at peace with that. We were really hoping that she could remain with us till the children are grown. That is not up to us.

Trace wants you to know that she loves you and appreciates everything you have done for her.

You can still send cards and letters to her if you like…but the family asks that I field the phone calls and visits at this time. She wants to spend time with the family. Thank you for being so good to my sister. You are special to both of us.

We returned home that night. I stayed with her 24/7…we were both determined that we would beat this and prove every doctor wrong. I made myself a make-shift sleeping bag on the floor right next to her bed. I gave her the medications that were prescribed. I made sure she drank plenty of fluids and I tried to make sure she ate something everyday. Her children helped tremendously when they were home. Katy spent a few nights with us in the bedroom watching Lifetime television. At first, Ginni looked as though she was doing well. But she steadily grew weaker as the days went by; unable to walk and unable to control her pain.

Ginni brought up the day our own mother died. She was concerned that her children would be there when she passed, and she remembered how devastated she was on that day in 1975. She asked me to promise to be with her every moment until she went "Home", and to make sure her children did not go through the same thing we did. I promised her. She asked that she not be alone when it happened. She needed someone on "this" side because she knew she'd have plenty of people on the other side to greet her. She said wanted to "see the angels" like her friend Jackie did before her death. It broke my heart to hear her talk that way, but I understood. Her last request was that I never gave up the fight against breast cancer, and to use whatever means I had, to help in any way I could; and of course, I promised.

Days went by and neither one of us got any sleep. Her pain was out of control and she needed me to help her push the button on her morphine pump every 15 minutes. She had nearly stopped eating so it was difficult getting her to take anything by mouth, much less any type of oral pain medications. On the morning of April 7, 2005, I called Granddaddy and asked if he would meet me at Ginni's house and help me get her to Portsmouth Naval Hospital. We needed to get her pain under control. He was there almost immediately. Granddaddy and I got her in the car. She hardly spoke, she was just in and out enough to let us know when the pain was too much. When we arrived at the hospital, Granddaddy and I lifted her into a wheelchair and took her into the emergency room. She seemed somewhat alert while we were wheeling her through the hospital. She was able to give me enough information to admit her into Portsmouth Naval Hospital. It all changed just hours later.

"No longer should I be afraid to die. Jesus suffered for me so that I would not have to spend eternity in Hell. I should be happy to know that when I die, God will take me home. My bonds have been broken."

"Rooftop Wisdom" (The Heart that Knows.)

The price of wisdom is often high, its lessons don't come cheap;
the insight gained on wisdom's road is the kind you'll need to keep.
The broken heart that has placed itself in the Father's loving care,
Is the heart that knows in the midst of tears, that God is always there.

When wisdom shouts from a rooftop, it has earned the right to speak;
the strength it took to climb that high is the opposite of weak.
Battle weary? Maybe so, but its voice can crack the sky.
For it has thundered through the storm, unashamed to question why.

Perhaps the "why?" is still unanswered, so they've learned to let it go,
and that's a journey in itself, to trust when you don't know.
For the heart that believes that in the valley, it will never be alone;
is the heart that knows to take its fears and lay them at God's throne.

The heart that is touched by "rooftop wisdom" is the heart that comprehends;
the most important treasures in life are your family and your friends.
"Things" and the "stuff" you accumulate are trivial in their worth,
for memories made with those you love...are the richest gifts on earth.

Perspectives change, priorities shift, when wisdom wins first place;
Taking time to hear the silence and slowing down your pace.
Pausing a moment to give a hug, turning a frown into a smile;
the simple gestures from the heart are the kind that are worthwhile.

"Rooftop wisdom" knows the value of saying "I love you";
it's so amazing the inner healing those three little words can do.
The heart that seeks reconciliation is the heart that dwells in peace,
and knows God's grace is still amazing and will bring a sweet release.

So when you hear some words of wisdom from a "rooftop" point of
view,
Just remember the road they've walked somewhere ahead of you.
The heart that sees beyond the clouds to the sunshine up above,
Is the heart that lives by faith alone in God's unfailing love.

© 2004 Merissa Lee Kelley

"Finally, as my illness seems to progress here, I understand that I am so truly blessed. Blessed in more ways than I will ever know. I have loving family, friends, and newfound sisters in this journey we call life. I appreciate your prayers of support and healing and please know that they are never taken for granted. If metastatic cancer can be beat, I'm sure love has something to do with it."

Today, I am truly blessed by:

I took Ginni to the emergency room at Portsmouth Naval Hospital around 7:30 on the morning of the 7th. Even though two weeks before doctors at National Institutes of Health said that she didn't have much time, I still didn't give up hope. I believed the doctors were wrong and I intended to prove it when I admitted her. I begged for more tests. I lied. I told doctors in ER that NIH in Bethesda wasn't sure if the cancer had actually spread to her liver and she needed more tests. Her oncologist at Portsmouth was in his office consulting with ER and concurred that Ginni was in liver failure when I brought her in. It didn't dawn on me at the time that doctors from NIH and Portsmouth had already discussed her prognosis. It still didn't stop me from trying to get her some help.

Ginni had given me a copy of her Last Will and Testament and Living Will two years before her death. I never read it because I never believed she would die before I did. It was only after her funeral that I actually read it. She had designated *me* to make any decisions for her in the event that she couldn't make them for herself. In the ER, I felt I was forced to make a decision that I didn't want to make. The attending physician, Dr. B, asked if I wanted him to resuscitate her in the event that her heart stopped. I said it was up to Ginni so he began to shake her in an attempt to get answers. She moaned slightly. He raised his voice, "Ms. Michek! Do you want us to take the paddles to you and beat your chest if your heart should stop?" He shook her harder. "Ms. Michek! Do-you-want-us-to-beat-you-in-the-chest-with-the-paddles-if-your-heart-should-stop?!" Her eyes were still closed but she said as loud as she could, "I done already told you!" He was ready to shake her again but I stopped him. I walked around to the other side of the bed and said lightly in her ear, "Ginni, do you want us to let you go or save you?" She whispered, "Yes." I said, "Save you?" She whispered again, "Yes." I nearly stared a hole through the doctor. "You heard her! Save her!" I hoped that I didn't misunderstand her but I'm sure if she were in my shoes, she would have done the same thing.

Granddaddy stayed with Ginni and me while we waited for Dr. B to return with a plan of action. He and I discussed Ginni's fight and will to live. I don't know if we were just deluding ourselves or if we were still trying to hang on to faith. We sat and stared at her and her vital statistics on the monitors. Her blood pressure was dropping little by little.

Nearly an hour later, Ginni's oncologist Dr. H arrived. It was then that he confirmed that Ginni was in liver failure and it wouldn't be long until she succumbed to the disease. He suggested that we take her to the 4th floor hospice unit, admit her and try to keep her as comfortable as possible. Unlike Dr. B, his demeanor was compassionate and apologetic. I understand Dr. B's position now, whereas then I thought he was totally heartless. He was attempting to stop her suffering by verbally shaking me into accepting the inevitable. He knew I lied about the doctor's prognosis at NIH. I just wish he had handled my feelings with some compassion. I might have been more receptive. But then again, maybe not. I'm sure I was in denial. Ginni's oncologist Dr. H arrived and told us that Ginni was suffering. We needed to make a decision as quickly as possible. (He also apologized for not getting her into the allogenic stem cell trial earlier.) Instead of making the decision on my own, I asked Dr. H to leave Granddaddy and me alone for a moment. Dr. H said he would return in 15 minutes for our decision. I looked long at Granddaddy. He was already in tears. "We have to let her go, don't we Granddaddy?"
"Yes." he said softly."

Ginni was taken to 4th floor hospice. It was a very large room meant to accommodate many family members, but it was only the two of us, as she requested. Granddaddy had gone home to make sure Grandma would not be alone when the time came. At 1:50 a.m. on April 8th, the nurse woke me from a deep slumber. It felt like it had been months since I slept for more than an hour, and it felt good to rest for a bit. "She's going now" the nurse said. I sat up on my bed which was drawn close to hers. My body and mind were numb. I grabbed her hand as her eyes flew open wide. She looked straight up to the ceiling for a moment. "Oh my Lord!" I said. "She sees angels!" In a moment, she closed her eyes again.

I had goose bumps with the thought of angels being in that very room with us. She took four more breaths and she was gone. As I sat there in awe, sadness, and disbelief, I felt as though I was being embraced. It was so real, yet no one was there! But I knew it was Ginni. It *had* to be her. She wanted to say goodbye. I didn't want to move. I didn't want to lose her embrace, but it was gone when the nurse sat down beside me and caressed my shoulders. I fixed my eyes to the window behind her bed. It started to rain at that very moment. I knew I had to compose myself for a brief moment so I could call her children, but I couldn't do it. I called my husband and asked him to go to the house and tell them in person. And bring them to the hospital if they wanted to come.

The funeral was beautiful. Just like Ginni. Most of her friends and family wore "pink" in her honor. Her favorite songs were sung and most of the people she adored paid tribute to her. Her eldest son wore his military dress greens; her daughter wore a spectacular pink dress and her youngest son with a pink tie and pink Converse tennis shoes. I was amazed how much I could see "a little bit of Ginni" in all three of her children. The last thing she wanted to do was to leave them, and watching them at her funeral broke my heart in a million pieces because there was nothing more I could do. It was over. Now, they have to go through exactly what Ginni and I experienced; the rest of their lives without their beloved mother.

Once we left the cemetery, I didn't want to go home. Too many memories were there waiting for me and I wasn't ready to face them just yet. Stormy suggested that we get a breast cancer ribbon tattooed on our ankles. I didn't think twice. After lunch, Stormy, Aunt Joan, Briland Bride and I went down to the tattoo parlor and did the deed; pink ribbons with Ginni's name on it.

I had no idea why I did it at first, but then I remembered the day that Ginni had a bizarre last minute impulse to get a tattoo. "I always wanted one," she said. "Why not?" She had taken Aunt Joan out to lunch at Golden Corral one afternoon and talked her into getting one. AJ didn't believe they were going to go through with it at first, but whenever Ginni had an idea to do something, she did it. AJ got a rose and Ginni got a cross draped with a pink ribbon.

For months after Ginni died, I went through the motions of existence. I ignored friends, family, co-workers…everybody. However, I didn't realize I was doing it. I went through anger, denial, tears, unbelief, numbness…you name the emotion, and I probably had it. Losing my best friend and confidante left me feeling completely empty. I cried, I begged, I pleaded with God to answer me. I was so angry with Him. When I finally could not take one more morsel, I looked up and I screamed loud enough for the neighborhood to hear, "Why did you make ME the stem cell match when she wasn't going to be able to use them anyway?" Just then, I felt God speak in my spirit…He said it was so we could have precious quality time together. We wouldn't have had it if I weren't the match. Ginni prayed to become closer with me and her prayer was answered. It took me months to believe that, but now, I have no doubt. I believe it with all my heart. God knew what He was doing. He knew it was Ginni's time to go home…and He gave me an awesome gift. Time alone with my sister…my best friend.

Nobody ever can replace her and I strongly believe for close to a year after her death, I was looking for that. I compared everyone to her. I'm told that this is a normal part of grief, but I had a difficult time accepting what was considered "normal." Fortunately, family and friends allowed me that crucial time to wake up and see that there are people who are still out there who are with me through the rest of my walk through life. They are good people who are strong just like her...but in their own unique way. Thank God I didn't alienate them so much that gave up on me forever.

In September of 2005, I was pretty darn positive that people were tired of my lamenting about missing my sister, so I basically started keeping my thoughts to myself. When country singer Andy Griggs came to Busch Gardens Williamsburg on September 10th, I interviewed him just before his concert. We talked about his song "If Heaven", and I told him how it reminded me of Ginni's last moments on earth. She wanted to see the angels before she left...and before she took her last breaths of life, her eyes flew open wide and she looked straight up toward heaven. The line from his song came in my mind after I witnessed her peaceful departure, "If that's what heaven's made of, you know I ain't afraid to die." How could I be? My precious passed so beautifully and peacefully, how could I NOT believe there was Heaven? Andy dedicated that song to Ginni that day, and he cried as he performed that song. He said he hoped that Ginni was smiling in Heaven. I know she was.

If one could believe that our loved ones visit us in our dreams, then this will come as no surprise. On the night of December 22nd, 2005, I dreamed that Ginni was walking the hallway passing the window of the Eagle studio. I knew it was her and jumped from my chair to greet her. As I opened the studio door, she stepped in and embraced me. She only said one word. She mentioned my ex-husband's first name, "Claus." As we continued to embrace, there was an incredible feeling of understanding between us. I've experienced understanding before, but not to this magnitude. It was an unexplainable feeling that was obviously not of this world. The dream was so powerful that I had to tell the Ya-Yas about it as soon as I woke up. What happened later that day was a complete shock.

I received a call from Claus' sister Sandy. She said he had died. I was in complete shock. Did Ginni try to prepare me? Claus and I didn't part on bad terms and we remained good friends. We had a beautiful daughter (Gabby) together and she was important enough to us to let bygones be bygones. Gabby adored him. He worshiped the ground she walked on. Two days before Christmas, I had the difficult task of telling her that her father passed away.

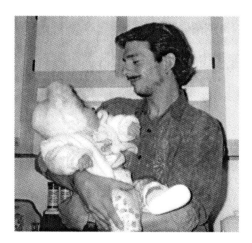

"I urge you to look at the relationships that you have in your life. Even the ones that looks broken. Is there something that you can do that could change the day of a person or heal

the wound of angry words. Can just a smile from you start a chain reaction that could reach around the world? Just think about it."

Thank you, Ginni! She could not have been more right about that. I value the friendship that Claus and I had even though we were divorced. And I value the love that his family still gives me to this day. I truly believe that Ginni came to tell me that Claus was okay. He had gone "Home" and he's there with her now. That is the only explanation for this dream. It was so real; it was like she and I were really embracing!   I can still remember every detail, including the clothes she was wearing. I have no doubt that God allowed her to see me for that brief moment for comfort. When I told his mother of this dream, I believe she found some peace in knowing that he was among people he loved.

Today, I am truly blessed by:

I had held up the promises that I made to Ginni except for one, and that was to do what it takes to continue fighting breast cancer. Frankly, for the first year after she died, I wasn't ready; but I tried to force myself anyway. It was a promise and I was going to keep it. My heart wasn't right, though. When you make a promise, you have to mean it. I was throwing myself into a charity without the proper motives. Did I really want to help fight breast cancer? Or did I foolishly believe if I worked hard enough, I could bring my sister back? The latter is true. I know it sounds silly, but it's true. I know I'm not the only person who has ever experienced this while dealing with grief.

October 2005, I planned to participate in the Tidewater Komen Affiliate's Race for a Cure. It took a survivor at one of the meetings to get real with me. She said I needed to take more time to grieve because my heart wasn't in it yet. She said I would know when I was ready and it will be then that I keep that promise. She was right and I am so grateful I listened, even though I was slightly offended at the time. This lady wasn't supposed to know how I felt. She was supposed to accept my offer to help. Fortunately, she didn't. I wouldn't have been much good to her at that time anyway. I believe she might have been in my shoes at some point in her life to be *that* observant.

As time passed, I read more and I researched more. The more I explored the issues of breast cancer education and detection, the more concerned I became. After years of believing otherwise, I learned first hand that breast cancer doesn't have to run in families, and it's not an "over 50" disease. I learned that an alarming number of women are not doing monthly self exams. Perhaps for the same reason I didn't do them in my early years? I don't know. It must be known that breast cancer knows no age, no race, no religion, no social status, and no gender! Something needs to be done and it starts with educating everyone about the latest breast cancer statistics and early detection. Then, I read Ginni's journals cover to cover...again. I am alarmed by what she experienced in the year prior to her breast cancer diagnosis. I became just angry enough to truly get out there and do my part to help educate as many people as I could about breast cancer, and to help raise funds to continue looking for a cure. In May of 2006, my heart was finally right to honor Ginni's request, and I was ready to move. I wasn't motivated by sadness anymore. I was motivated out of true concern. I became excited at the prospect of helping our local Komen Affiliate. The reason I chose Komen is because of a suggestion from Ginni's lead transplant doctor at National Institutes of Health. I am grateful that he is still available to answer questions when I ask. When I was still in the grieving stage, I asked him via email to help me decide which breast cancer organization to donate my time to. He said that all of the organizations are wonderful, but Komen had done the most to encourage women to explore clinical trials. While I am sad that the clinical trial did not work for Ginni, what they learned from the both of us *will* benefit someone else. Another woman's sister will live because of Ginni and me. I am at peace knowing this.

John Shomby suggested that I organize The Eagle's on-air Breast Cancer Awareness Month campaign. Our promotions department purchased a beautiful electric pink guitar and we had taken it to concerts throughout the year to get autographed by some of country's top selling female artists. We auctioned this guitar on our website for Tidewater Komen. I took on the duty as The Eagle's team captain for the 2006 Tidewater Komen Affiliate Race for the Cure. I was so excited because it was the beginning of honoring my promise to Ginni. I didn't get my hopes up too high. I figured we'd start out with a small team and work our way up over the next couple of years or so.

I was totally surprised by the awesome show of love and support from not only my family and co-workers, but Eagle listeners, Ginni's friends and Ya-Yas. That little miracle convinced me that I was finally ready to continue what she started. What I anticipated to be a small team was actually the LARGEST corporate team at the Race! So many people who learned of Ginni's story through the local news, radio, newspaper and the internet joined the team. And Ya-Yas signed up to be "Spirit Runners" and contributed to the cause as well! When I was handed the award for the Largest Corporate Team, I held it up because I wanted to make sure Ginni saw it. "Look Ginni! It's happening! We're doing it!" And I can SWEAR I heard her say, "Yes, we are."

Steph Snode from the Tidewater Affiliate of the Susan G. Komen Foundation and Karen

"More than Ever"

In every season of my life, my God has seen me through
The tears, the joys, the ups and downs; have all been in His view
His faithfulness is timeless and He gives me wings to fly
But more than ever, He held me near when I had to say good-bye

He knows that grief can overwhelm, and He understands our tears
He knows "uncharted territory" can multiply our fears
I've learned He "overwhelms" the grief with peace beyond compare

Which brings you joy to know He has your loved one in His care
Wrapped within God's arms of grace, I found the strength to see
How precious in the sight of God, is His child who's finally free
Free from pain and earthly bonds free to soar above

Free to run with hands outstretched into God's arms of love
I knew there never was a moment that Ginni walked alone
God led her through the shadowed valley to kneel before His throne
But death is just a fleeting journey to those who've made the choice

To live for Christ with all their heart and listen for his voice
Because of Christ, the "good-byes" we speak are not the final say
It's such a joy to have the hope of a sweet reunion day
Ginni's eyes saw Heaven and God saw Ginni, a daughter who won
the race

And more than ever I truly saw the treasure of His grace
It's good to know the loving arms that held my sister tight
Will keep me close within His reach so I'll stay in His sight
And more than ever I understand His sovereign will is best
For to be a part of Ginni's life has made my life so blessed

© *2005, Merissa Lee Kelley*

Today, I am truly blessed by:

On Monday, November 6, I kept my appointment at the Diagnostic Center where my original mammogram was performed. I was praying that there would be no lump visible in the upcoming set of films, and perhaps it was there because I accidentally moved when the picture was taken. I was not that lucky. Not only was the lump evident in the mammogram, it was further seen in the ultrasound. Not a good sign, but still not conclusive of anything serious. My doctor requested a biopsy of the problem area as soon as possible.

Strangely enough, I was not as frightened as I thought I'd be. I'll attempt to explain it. The last three years of Ginni's life, I watched her, I listened to her and I know the questions to ask. I've met dozens of breast cancer survivors who were more than willing to answer every question I ever had about the disease. I was a caregiver once. I stayed on top of every chemo Ginni received. I learned about new treatments. I read about every clinical trial dedicated to breast cancer research. (A lot of great treatments have been discovered since Ginni was initially diagnosed.) Besides all of that, I asked the Ya-Yas and my co-workers for prayer, and I truly believe I could feel them.

I've heard of the problems some women face when coordinating their health care. Fortunately, Ginni was a military dependent so she didn't have to worry about hefty hospital bills in order to continue her treatment, but I learned the hard way about examining my insurance plan carefully concerning my benefits. I have been going to the same doctor for years and I trust him. He always keeps a watchful eye on me, especially now since breast cancer *is* in my family. Naturally, I went to the center he referred me to for my mammogram. I had a slight out-of-pocket payment for the procedure, but it was worth it to stay ahead of the game. I didn't realize that this center was out of my insurance company's network because I didn't read over my plan carefully. I discovered this after I made the appointment for the biopsy at that same facility. The business office called and briefed me of what my out of pocket costs would be if I chose to have the procedure done there. This was a wake up call. I should have thought ahead about my health care especially with something as significant as what I was going through. Fortunately, an agent at my insurance company led me in the right direction, but because I didn't check my benefits before the mammogram, I had to begin from scratch and locate a hospital in my network to perform the follow-up mammograms and biopsy. With help and diligence, I was able to secure an appointment at an in-network hospital for the 14th of November. The sad thing was, I wasted 48 hours by not keeping myself informed about changes in my plan. The upside of my error, well, maybe God allowed me to experience this little setback so I can help someone else. And if it does help at least one person, mission accomplished. So I have this advice for everyone, good health or not so good. Read over your insurance policy again and make sure you know what's covered and where it is covered. Stay on top of any changes in your benefits, and always ask questions. You will get answers if you ask. And if you don't understand any area of your policy, again, ask the questions. Once I read through my insurance plan again and asked my provider some simple questions, I had no trouble getting my appointments and my co-pays in order. For those who cannot afford health insurance or cannot get it for one reason or another, some health care providers offer "Uninsured Patient Discount Programs." Take the time to find out where they are and if you qualify.

November 14th, 2006, I had a Stereotactic Breast Biopsy and it wasn't as bad as I thought it would be. There was only minor discomfort, but not enough that I wasn't able to handle it. The mammograms were 100 times worse than the biopsy, in my opinion. The procedure itself doesn't take long. It's actually the preparation that takes most of the time. Since the needle was going to be guided by mammogram, I had to be situated in the right position. I was awake during the procedure. I was lying on my stomach and my right breast was placed through an opening on the operating table. Underneath this table was a paddle-shaped mammogram instrument that was used to locate the lump. After the lump was found, the doctor injected a local anesthetic in the breast. Once the area was numb, she inserted the biopsy needle, using the mammogram pictures as a guide, to lift tissue samples from the mass. The most uncomfortable part of the procedure for me was a little shoulder cramp from the position I was lying in. Nurse Martha helped keep my mind off of the procedure by quizzing me about the "Faith Hill Debacle" at the Country Music Association Awards show from the previous week. (Faith was nominated for Female Vocalist of the Year, and when newcomer Carrie Underwood took the win, Faith displayed discontent on camera. Word is, Faith was just joking because she knew the camera was on.) I told Martha that after watching the video several times, I really believed she was just kidding around. That conversation must have taken 5 minutes, and by the time we finished chatting, the biopsy was all finished.

I was instructed to keep ice packs on the area for at least 24 hours, and rest. I had absolutely no problem with that. I figured it would give me ample time to catch up on some Lifetime television! The hardest part was the 48 hour wait for the diagnosis, but my mind was eased by reading Ginni's journals front and back, over and over, several times…again. I always find inspiration in them and I found this one that helped right after the biopsy:

"If we make a choice to pray instead of worry, we will personally experience God's peace. What a promise!"

"Lord, when people look at me and what I'm going through, let them see You in it. Amen."

I repeated those lines over and over. How calming they were. I made a choice to pray. I thanked God for His answer, no matter what it was. I asked God to let others see Him in me. Wow, I really sounded like Ginni! I knew how she felt; keeping my faith on Him and not on the situation.   Then, I closed my eyes and went to sleep.

I'm really thrilled to say that my insurance company and the medical community is really on top of educating the public about early detection, and they didn't play around when a suspicious mass was found. Once I understood my part in the process and took measures, they were thorough. They made sure that everything was completed from beginning to end. During my biopsy, the doctor placed markers around the lump just in case if wasn't cancer, so they could keep their eye on that area in particular with subsequent mammograms. The markers are on the mass itself, so it is only seen on a mammo or x-ray. I had never heard of this practice before, but thought it was an awesome idea. It gives me a little extra peace of mind.

November 16th, 2006, it was a long day to say the least. For days since before the biopsy, I maintained a level head. I didn't stress about the impending diagnosis. However, the first thing that morning, I couldn't eat breakfast; I had a nervous stomach and my head was pounding. I didn't understand why. For some strange reason, I could not control the anxiety no matter how many deep breaths I took. A warm shower calmed me slightly. Enough to get dressed and make the 45 minute drive to the station. Once I got there, the anxiety kicked in again, but I tried not to let it show. I couldn't understand why I had been so good up until that morning.

Our annual radiothon for Union Mission's Feed the Hungry campaign was happening that day. Most of the show was spent raising funds to help our local homeless shelter. I think that radiothon could not have come at a better time. With a representative going on the air with me with updates every 15 minutes, I was able to keep my mind off of the phone call that I was supposed to receive right around lunch hour. The representative and I shared stories about those who had gone from having nothing to having hope. Before long, my mind was completely off of the phone call and on that word we kept saying on the air … "hope." And I loved saying that word, because it reminded me of the night that Ginni reassured us with these words, "There is always hope." Once again, I was calm, just as I was before I woke up that morning.

Right at 1 p.m., I got a call on my cell. I couldn't answer it because I was preparing to talk with the Union Mission representative again, but I recognized the number as being that of the hospital. I let it go to voicemail. Whatever the diagnosis, it waited this long; it can wait another few minutes. Ten minutes later, I took a deep breath, and then checked the messages. It was the nurse. "Your biopsy results are back. Everything is fine. The tumor is benign. We'll see you again at your next mammogram." I looked up and thanked God for his blessing. I thanked the Ya-Yas and my friends and co-workers for their continued prayers. And I thanked Ginni for being my inspiration. Without her, her strong faith and will to live, I think I'd still be living in the dark as I did in my early years. Ginni would say that I am still a "Dork", but I think she's proud that I'm a much smarter dork. Amen.

Today, I am truly blessed by:

"I didn't ask for cancer; it asked for me. I chose not to give into it but I can't deny how it has changed me for the better."
- Virginia "Ginni" Michek 10/10/62 - 04/08/05
http://www.tracesjourney.com

June 2000

It's been quite some time since I have updated "my story". Much has happened. Some good. Some not so good.

I opted for the prophylactic mastectomy and had it done. It wasn't bad at all. As a matter of fact, I took my Statistics final for college with my drainage tube dangling on a pin from my sweat pants. In no time I was back up on my feet and college graduation rolled around.

I earned my Associates Degree in Applied Science in May of last year. My, how time flies! I found a job in the contested Family Law section of a law firm here in town. I love my job. Perhaps not the contested matters that I see every day, but I love the part where I get to help people sort out their lives. It's a challenge every day but isn't life itself a challenge?

My husband, a military Non Commissioned Officer, ended up on orders for Korea on a year unaccompanied tour in August of last year. The kids and I began our routine of school, work, and shuffling busy schedules while missing a husband and father. We definitely had our plates full. :-)

I was worried about him being gone so far for so long and had prayed that God would not let him go if something would happen to me while he was gone. (I always had this 'fear' that the cancer would come back) Since he ended up leaving, I believed that God would watch over me and the kids. He did, but not in the way I had planned. Of course, God's plans are not our own.

I had a 'routine' oncology visit in March of this year. Nothing was routine about it. I was five years out of initial diagnosis but something was amiss. I had my normal pre-appointment blood tests and the only abnormality was the ever present low red blood cells. My onc and I discussed my fatigue and the fact that my hair was coming out. Of course stress could be a factor, however I had lost a little bit of weight. Again, stress from having to handle things on my own? The onc ordered the CA 27-29 test and a thyroid test. To make a long story short, a couple of weeks later I had a CA 27-29 result of 54, whereas in the past the results hung out at around 21. I immediately saw my favorite surgeon, Dr. W. understandably in great anguish at the results. Dr. W. ordered a bone scan and another CA 27-29. This time the results were 60. Lab error? Bone scan showed "uptake" in the left sacrum and sternum, but not conclusive for bone mets. He then ordered a CAT scan which showed no abnormality, however the ever diligent Dr. W. ordered an MRI of the two bone areas in question. The MRI's stated presumed bone mets but without a bone biopsy nothing could be 100 percent certain. It was certain to me though that the cancer was back. Since my initial tumor was estrogen positive, when I saw the oncologist, I was offered the option of removing the ovaries in the hopes of slowing any growth that may be occurring in the bones. Once the ovaries were removed, mets were found in the left ovary, thus no need for a bone biopsy to confirm mets. The cancer was for sure back.

I am at the road now as to determine 'treatment'. Since May first when the gyn doc told me about confirmed mets to the ovary, I've been researching. I see the onc again who suggested the ovary removal on the 13th and I think I'm going with Arimidex and Aredia. Only time will tell if that will keep me 'stable'.

As far as having the ovaries removed, I am doing remarkably well (in my opinion) in that I have suffered no hot flashes or any of the other 'horrible' things I heard that could happen. I am somewhat irritable, but I'm on a low dose antidepressant to hopefully keep that under control. I hear too that low dose antidepressants combat hot flashes. Only time will tell. Plus, who wouldn't be irritable at a time like this. :-)

I am back at work and my husband is home from Korea on a 'compassionate reassignment'. It's good he is home for my goofy mood swings and to help the kids cope. As far as he coping? He's not shared a whole lot with me, which leads me to believe that he is bumbling through it right now like I am. This too shall pass........

So, for now, "The cancer may get me, but it's going to have to catch me first!" I'm off on a new road God is leading me down.

July 2000

This month has just flown by! Last month I mentioned perhaps asking the oncologist about doing Arimidex and Aredia. Well, I guess we are still going to hold off on deciding about any further hormonal manipulation until next month. I had my ovaries removed in May and this past CA 27-29 test showed a decrease of seven points. I am back down to 60. Since my knowledge of the mets, the marker has been 54, 60, 67 and now 60. Certainly a CA 27-29 result of 60 is not 'normal', yet it is worthy of praise to God for a trend in the right direction. Perhaps it is an indication that the cancer cells are responding to their lack of 'fuel'. :-) I read on the listservs where I subscribe of people having by far worse tumor marker results and can't help but feel blessed. I pray for continued response to treatment.

Speaking of listservs, I have been thinking a lot about the relation between the net and treatment. Clearly through experiences of others I have met on the net and the research of many wonderful sites, I have become a very 'informed' patient. I have read of an unfortunate incident where a patient showed her oncologist discussions and research on the net which might be of positive result to her and the oncologist balked at and dismissed this patients' feelings and concerns by insinuating the net consists of a bunch of quackery. This oncologist suggested that if something wasn't written about in Medical Journals, then she would not even dispense of the time to discuss it.

Hold up one minute here. I was mortified in reading this!! On one hand I completely understand that the net DOES consist of an element of 'quackery'. I completely understand that I am not the only patient my oncologist treats and that s/he can't spend two hours discussing the latest in internet 'cures'. I completely understand that an oncologist or any doctor would be and SHOULD be very hesitant to prescribe a treatment without thoroughly researching the validity of the claim. What I DON'T understand is the arrogance and Almighty God attitude of some doctors. This is MY life that is in their hands and "I" am in charge of MY healthcare. If I die, it won't be the doctor that treated me in Eternity.....it would be me. I believe that if it is my ultimate decision to put a DNR on my chart, then it should be my decision to decide which treatment, if any, that is offered to try or go AMA if my heart tells me different then that of science.

I believe that the proper response of the above oncologist should have been to take the printed out claims that the patient brought to her visit and review them at the oncologist's leisure. Perhaps tell the patient that at the next visit they will discuss her finding. Make it the two way street that it is. I believe that the net can be both helpful and harmful to the medical community but with an effort between patient AND doctor, the bad weeds can be eliminated and new, more beneficial growth can abound for all.

So, enough of my Soap Box. :-) I wish you all well and may your days be blessed.

THINGS TO MAKE YOU THINK

THIS LETTER WAS WRITTEN BY GOD TO US!

You may not know me, but I know everything about you...
Psalm 139:1
I know when you sit down and when you rise up...
Psalm 139:2
I am familiar with all your ways...
Psalm 139:3
Even the very hairs on your head are numbered...
Matthew 10:29-31
For you were made in my image...
Genesis 1:27
In me you live and move and have your being...

Acts 17:28

For you are my offspring....

Acts 17:28

I knew you even before you were conceived...

Jeremiah 1:4-5

I chose you when I planned creation...

Ephesians 1: 11-12

You were not a mistake, for all your days are written in my book...

Psalm 139:15-16

I determined the exact time of your birth and where you would live...

Acts 17:26

You are fearfully and wonderfully made...

Psalm 139:14

I knit you together in your mother's womb...

Psalm 139:13

And brought you forth on the day you were born...

Psalm 71:6

I have been misrepresented by those who don't know me...

John 8:41-44

I am not distant and angry, but am the complete expression of love...

I John 4:16

And it is my desire to lavish my love on you simply because you are my

child and I am your father...

1 John 3:1

I offer you more than your earthly father ever could...

Matthew 7:11

For I am the perfect father...

Matthew 5:48

Every good gift that you receive comes from my hand...

James 1:17

For I am your provider and I meet all your needs...

Matthew 6:31-33

My plan for your future has always been filled with hope...

Jeremiah 29:11

Because I love you with an everlasting love...

Jeremiah 31:3

My thoughts towards you are countless as the sand on the seashore...

Psalm 139:17-18

And I rejoice over you with singing...
Zephaniah 3:17
I will never stop doing good to you...
Jeremiah 32:40
For you are my treasured possession...
Exodus 19:5
I desire to establish you with all my heart and all my soul...
Jeremiah 32:41
And I want to show you great and marvelous things...
Jeremiah 33:3
If you seek me with all your heart, you will find me...
Deuteronomy 4:29
Delight in me and I will give you the desires of your heart...
Psalm 37:4
For it is I who gave you those desires...
Philippians 2:13
I am able to do more for you than you could possibly imagine...
Ephesians 3:20
For I am your greatest encourager...
2 Thessalonians 2:16-17
I am also the Father who comforts you in all your troubles...
2 Corinthians 1:3-4
When you are brokenhearted, I am close to you...
Psalm 34:18
As a shepherd carries a lamb, I have carried you close you my heart...
Isaiah 40:11
One day I will wipe away every tear from your eyes and will take away all
the pain you have suffered on this earth....
Revelation 21:3-4
I am your Father, and I love you even as I love my son, Jesus...
John 17:23
For in Jesus, my love for you is revealed...
John 17:26
He is the exact representation of my being...
Hebrews 1:3
He came to demonstrate that I am for you, not against you...
Romans 8:31
And to tell you that I am not counting your sins...

2 Corinthians 5:18-19
Jesus died so that I could be reconciled...
2 Corinthians 5:18-19
His death was the ultimate expression of my love for you...
I John 4:10
I gave up everything I loved that I might gain your love...
Romans 8:38-39
Come home and I'll throw the biggest party heaven has ever seen...
Luke 15:7
I have always been Father, and will always be Father...
Ephesians 3:14-15
My question is ... Will you be my child?
John 1:12-13
I am waiting for you ...
Luke 15:11-32

MORE.....

IS THERE A ROCK IN YOUR SANDBOX?

A little boy was spending his Saturday morning playing in his sand box. He
had with him his box of cars and trucks, his plastic pail, and a shiny,
red plastic shovel.

In the process of creating roads and tunnels in the soft sand, he
discovered a large rock in the middle of the sand box!

The boy dug around the rock, managing to dislodge it from the sand. With
no little bit of struggle, he pushed and nudged the rock across the
sandbox by using his feet. (He was a very small boy and the rock was very
huge.) When the boy got the rock to the edge of the sandbox, however, he

found that he couldn't roll it up and over the little wall. Determined, the little boy shoved, pushed, and pried, but every time he had made some
progress, the rock tipped and then fell back into the sand box.

The little boy grunted, struggled, pushed, and shoved; but his only reward
was to have the rock roll back, smashing his chubby fingers. Finally he burst into tears of frustration. All this time the boy's father watched from his living room window as the drama unfolded.

The moment the tears fell, a large shadow fell across the boy and the sandbox. It was the boy's father.

Gently but firmly he said, "Son, why didn't you use all the strength that you had available?" Defeated, the boy sobbed back, "But I did Daddy, I did! I used all the strength that I had!"

"No, son," corrected the father kindly, "you didn't use all the strength you had. You didn't ask me."

With that the father reached down, picked up the rock, and removed it from
the sandbox.

There is One who is always available to us and willing to give us all the strength we need. "When you are DOWN to nothing.... God is UP to something!"

"Faith sees the invisible, Believes the incredible, And receives the impossible!!"

"Doubts see the obstacles, Faith sees beyond them."

Thank you Sharon & Ray!

August 2000

Well, here we are midway into August. Time sure flies. I had my oncologist appointment on the 8th and have good news to report. My CA 27-29 was down to 45! Last month it was 60 so it seems the hormonal 'manipulation' is working -or better -the decline of hormones is working. I started Arimidex on the 9th. It is my understanding that Arimidex is another anti-estrogen type drug similar to Tamoxifen. Another name for it is Anastrozole and the goal is to reduce even further the estrogen floating around in my fat cells (ugh) and starve the little hormone hungry cancer cells to death. What estrogen was left from removing the ovaries will hopefully get caught with the Arimidex.

On the 11th I started Aredia. Another name for it is Pamidronate and it is not a chemotherapy. Aredia touts that it helps regulate blood calcium levels and aids in the treatment of bone loss. It is given via infusion-YIKES! My mother in law went with me for my treatment and as soon as the chemo nurse hooked me up to the IV, my mother in law and I toted the IV pole around the hospital for 2 hours. It was great! I was able to work with my anxiety and reduce it by walking in and out of the hospital, and was able to pass the time in good, lively conversation. Plus I drank two Gatorades! How much better could a treatment get? *Smile*

So far (and I do not anticipate) I have not had any ill effects from either drug. I say about 50 times a day, "I'm tired," however those words have fallen off my lips many times in the past 6 years and even before -when our babies came along. *grin* I cannot blame the tiredness on low red blood cells any more either as they seem to have come up. Believe it or not, I cannot recall a time in recent history where my red blood cells were in that 'normal' range. So, all in all though, I seem to be doing quite well and I am reminded every day how truly blessed I am whether 'tired' or not.

On the 16th of this month it will be 6 years since I was diagnosed with cancer. I am in awe of the progress in treatment since initially hearing the words, "it's malignant." I believe there will come a day when cancer is like diabetes; a treatable disease. Until that day, I plug on.........

SEPTEMBER 2000

IT'S SORT OF FUNNY WRITING MY SEPTEMBER UPDATE ON THE LAST DAY OF THE MONTH. THERE HAS BEEN NO REAL CHANGE IN MY STATUS THOUGH. I'M STILL PLUGGIN' ON.........
I WAS HAVING MY HAIR DONE A COUPLE OF WEEKS AGO AND READ AN ARTICLE IN ONE OF THE WOMENS MAGAZINES ABOUT FORD AND THEIR 'RACE FOR THE CURE'. NOW GRANTED, FORD ISN'T A POPULAR NAME RIGHT NOW IN LIGHT OF THE FIRESTONE TIRE DEAL, HOWEVER I OWN TWO FORDS SO I'M KIND OF PARTIAL. :-) ANYWAY, THERE'S THIS SUPPOSED CONTEST AT THEIR SITE FOR SURVIVORS CALLED 'FRESH START FOR SURVIVORS'. JUST FOR GIGGLES, THIS IS WHAT I WROTE.......

I've heard that the mind and the heart both have individual memories. I've learned it's the heart memories that tug at and free the spirit of life and living. I am a thirty-seven-year old military wife, mother to three precious children, and a six-year survivor of breast cancer. I've lived a cranium full of the typical memories of births, deaths, graduations, moves and equal milestones. Recently I have been diagnosed with early metastasis to the bone. Strangely I am learning something with this diagnosis that I didn't quite grasp the first go round on this ride named cancer---that each and every second of life is so very, very, endearingly special. The smile, the touch, the words, the smells of some of the most everyday of things construct fiercely tender heart memories: the sideways glance of a chastised child; the challenging yet wobbled stance of teenage independence; a tiny hand wiping a tear over the lost ball game; a smudge of jelly, again, on the cabinet; the smell of a wet dog and little boy; a plea for help with homework; the incessant ringing of a telephone with the sound of clamoring feet to answer it; a yawn and tosseled hair at breakfast; and the whispered giggles that fall with the night. Each and every second is a new spirit lifting memory to the heart and a second worth celebrating.

NOW, I HARDLY THINK I WILL 'WIN' ANYTHING, HOWEVER SOMETHING PROMPTED ME TO WRITE WHAT I WAS FEELING AT THE MOMENT. I'VE BEEN KNOWN TO BE PRETTY TENDER HEARTED, HOWEVER AS OF LATE, I'M EVEN SURPRISING MYSELF AT THE THINGS THAT SORT OF TUG AT MY HEART. IT'S ODD....I DON'T BELIEVE I AM AS QUICK TO CRY AT THINGS BUT I AM QUICKER TO FEEL (AS IF THAT MADE SENSE). MAYBE EVERY ONE WHO HAS EVER THOUGHT THEY HAD IT BAD IN LIFE SHOULD STEP INSIDE THE HEART OF ONE WITH A SERIOUS ILLNESS.....IF ONLY FOR A SECOND OF A GLIMPSE. PERHAPS THEY WOULD SEE THE WORLD IN A DIFFERENT LIGHT. IF GIVEN THE RIGHT PERSPECTIVE, LIFE IS NOT ALL THAT BAD.
TILL NEXT MONTH.............

October 2000

Well, here it is already mid-October. Not only is the amount of daylight getting shorter, the days seem to be getting shorter too. You know what they say.....time flies when you are having fun!
In case you were not aware, it is Breast Cancer Awareness Month. The push for a mammogram is everywhere. Can you stand another push?

The American Cancer Society provides a great explanation about mammography, the exam, tips and what to expect. Check it out if you have not already done so. I know, I know,......you are thinking, "hey wait, YOUR tumor did not show up on a mammogram." Ok, so you got me and you are soooo right, HOWEVER, I am not the norm and neither are you. In my NON medical opinion, there is NO norm. Besides, mammography is a good diagnostic tool, however not the ONLY tool in gauging breast health. Your doctor will know more....why not call and make that appointment now?

I sound like a soundbite, huh? Just wait till next month.....ELECTION month. Whoooohoooo! Ok, I promise to be nice....maybe. Back to serious....and soundbites.

www.friendsinneed.com

If you have checked out some of my links, you may have already seen Susan's page, Friends In Need. A great bunch of ladies here. If you are new to breast cancer and are in need of support, Susan has it. If you have metastatic disease and are in need of support, Susan has it. This was my first online support group and they have helped me immensely. If you have time, check it out, join the chats, meet others who are battling this disease.

Now, this page belongs to Karen. It's pretty cool in that she shares EVERYTHING. Anything and everything you always wanted to know about breast cancer, but were afraid to ask. She's pretty awesome too in that she writes just like she is talking to you in person.

In case you have not guessed it by now....I am a Christian. This group is Christian oriented and is absolutely wonderful in offering prayers and poems of support. Even if you are not a Christian, you still may find comfort and friendship in this loving environment. Check it out.

NOVEMBER 2000

WELL HERE IT IS, THE END OF NOVEMBER. IT HAS BEEN
A MONTH OF BLESSINGS, BIG AND SMALL, AND A TIME
TO TRULY SIT BACK AND REFLECT ON ALL THAT I HAVE
AND TO GIVE THANKS. THERE IS A SIGN ON MY WAY TO
WORK THAT READS, "THOSE WHO DON'T THANK
FOR A LITTLE, WON'T THANK FOR A LOT". I AM
REMINDED THAT WE SIMPLY HAVE NO IDEA OF JUST
HOW MUCH WE HAVE. IT IS EASY TO THANK GOD FOR
THE ROOF OVER OUR HEAD, THE FOOD ON THE
TABLE AND CLOTHES ON OUR BACKS...BUT DO WE? ARE
THOSE SIMPLY A 'GIVEN' IN LIFE? EVERY MORNING
WHEN I GET UP, I THANK GOD FOR ALLOWING ME
TO TAKE MY FIRST CONSCIOUS PAIN FREE BREATH
OF THE DAY. I AM ACUTELY AWARE OF THE THINGS
I USE TO TAKE FOR GRANTED. NOW YOU M AY SAY THAT
BREATHING IS NOT SOMETHING ONE WOULD TAKE FOR
GRANTED. AND YOU MAY BE RIGHT, BUT I NEVER
GAVE A WHOLE LOT OF THOUGHT THAT I WAS
ALLOWED YET ANOTHER DAY TO BREATHE..AND FOR
THAT I AM MOST THANKFUL. FOR WITH THAT BREATH, I
CAN
SAY, 'I LOVE YOU' TO THOSE CLOSE TO ME, I CAN USE THAT
BREATH TO SAY WORDS OF COMFORT OR
ENCOURAGEMENT
TO THOSE WHO NEED TO HEAR IT THE MOST. I CAN USE
THAT
BREATH TO WHISPER WORDS OF PRAISE AND WORSHIP TO
THE GOD WHO SO GRACIOUSLY GAVE HIS SON SO THAT I
MAY LIVE.
YES, I AM ETERNALLY THANKFUL!!

ON A MEDICAL REPORT, MY CA 27-29 TUMOR MARKER
FELL THIS MONTH TO 33. MY PRAYER AND THE PRAYER I
HAD

ASKED OF SO MANY,
WAS TO HAVE A COUNT OF 38, WHICH IS THE UPPER END
OF 'NORMAL'. WELL, NOT MY WILL BUT GOD'S WILL, AND
GOD'S WILL WAS EVEN BETTER!! THANK YOU ALL FOR
YOUR PRAYERS AND WORDS OF SUPPORT.

UNTIL NEXT MONTH, CHECK OUT THIS SITE:
DrSavard.com

CHRISTMAS 2000

IT'S HERE!!!! CHRISTMAS EVE. I GUESS THE KIDS NEVER
THOUGHT IT WOULD GET HERE. I REMEMBER THOSE
DAYS..DREAMING OF WHAT WAS UNDER THE TREE. I
REMEMBER WANTING A GUITAR (THOUGH I COULD NOT
AND STILL CANNOT PLAY). I REMEMBER WANTING A
STUFFED BEAR THAT PLAYED MUSIC--A SCOTTY BEAR I
CALLED IT (ALTHOUGH I WAS 17--NOT 7). BUT WHAT I
REMEMBER MOST THOUGH WAS NOT BEING ABLE TO
SLEEP THAT NIGHT. HMMMM. SOME THINGS NEVER
CHANGE....**GRIN**

MY CHRISTMAS PRESENT CAME EARLY THIS YEAR. IF YOU
REMEMBER LAST MONTH, MY CA 27-29 WAS 33--BELOW THE
COVETED 38. THAT IS AWESOME. WELL, I HAD AN MRI
STUDY OF THE BONE IN QUESTION. IT APPEARS THAT
THERE IS NO SIGN OF CANCER THERE. I WAS STUNNED AT
THE NEWS. THRILLED MIND YOU BUT MORE SO STUNNED.
WHAT DO YOU MEAN THERE IS NO SIGN OF CANCER
THERE? WHERE DID IT GO?

I'VE BEEN READING DR. CHARLES STANLEY'S "THE WONDERFUL SPIRIT FILLED LIFE" HE SAYS TO LOOK EVERY DAY FOR EVIDENCE OF GOD'S SUPERNATURAL INTERVENTION. NOW THAT I HAVE REALLY STARTED TO LOOK FOR IT, I CAN SEE IT, FEEL IT, HEAR IT, TASTE IT. HIS INTERVENTION IS EVERYWHERE....WE JUST HAVE TO TAKE OUR EYES OFF OF THE BIG THINGS THAT CLUTTER OUR THOUGHTS. IT'S IN MISSING THE TRAFFIC BY 1 MINUTE-- NOT IN THE ONE HOUR COMMUTE TO WORK, WATCHING THE SUN COME UP-- NOT THE SMOG SETTLE IN, IT'S IN LISTENING TO THE BIRDS SONG--NOT THE NOISE OF THE DAY SILENCING THEIR TUNE, IT'S IN THE FIRST FRUIT OF THE TREE--NOT THE LEAVES THAT FALL. IT'S EVERYWHERE AND WE ARE JUST TOO CLUTTERED TO NOTICE IT.

WELL ON THIS CHRISTMAS EVE, I AM REMINDED OF ALL THOSE GIFTS FROM HIM BY THE BIRTH OF A TINY BABY. SOME OF HIS BEST GIFTS COME IN THE SMALLEST OF PACKAGES. FOR EVIDENCE OF GOD'S INTERVENTION WE NEED TO LOOK AT THE SUBTLE THINGS. ONCE WE LOOK THERE, WE WILL SEE HIM EVERYWHERE.

MAY YOU HAVE A JOYOUS AND MERRY CHRISTMAS!!!

DECEMBER 26, 2000

Good morning everyone! I hope this day after the BIG celebration finds you all well and at peace. This Christmas was even more bittersweet for me. I didn't want to open my gifts as much as I wanted to watch the faces of my family. That meant more to me than anything anyone could have given to me. I wrote those faces on the memory of my heart never to be forgotten, even on the the bleakest of days my future may hold. I am reminded that the present is a present sent from God to be cherished more than any tomorrow I may receive.

We had our birthday cake to Jesus made this year and it was beautiful! As we sang Happy Birthday to Jesus, I imagined Him blowing out the candles and making a wish that we would all desire His gift that was hung on the Tree before all others under the tree.

My prayer for you all is that you accept the healing God has for your heart for today. Hugz!!!

JANUARY 2001

WELCOME TO THE NEW YEAR!! MY PRAYER IS THAT THIS IS THE YEAR FOR A MAJOR ADVANCEMENT IN THE TREATMENT OF METASTATIC BREAST CANCER. I LOST A FRIEND JUST A FEW DAYS AGO, BUT GOD HAS GAINED AN AWESOME SMILE TO ADD TO THE BEAUTY OF HEAVEN.

MY LIVER SCAN TURNED OUT TO BE PRETTY GOOD. THERE WAS A NODULE NOTED SOME TIME AGO, BUT AFTER A FEW FANCY DANCY SCANS ALONG THE WAY, THAT NODULE IS SAID TO BE NOTHING BUT A HEMANGIOMA. KNOWING WHAT IT IS SORT OF EASES MY MIND A BIT IN THAT I WOULD LIKE TO KEEP THE CANCER CELLS OUT OF VITAL ORGANS FOR AS LONG AS I CAN--TRANSLATE-FOREVER. =)

AS YOU ARE AWARE BY NOW, I SUBSCRIBE TO SEVERAL LISTSERVS. BELOW IS AN ARTICLE WRITTEN BY A YOUNG LADY ON THE METASTATIC BREAST CANCER WEB SITE. ABSOLUTELY FANTASTIC IF YOU WANT TO KNOW HOW TO REALLY HELP SOMEONE WHO IS BATTLING THIS DISEASE. THANK YOU TRISHA FOR ALLOWING ME TO PLACE SUCH WONDERFUL INSIGHT ON MY SITE AND THANK YOU

READER FOR YOUR INTEREST IN HELPING THOSE WHO ARE STRUGGLING WITH THIS ILLNESS.

TILL NEXT MONTH!

What Can You Do For Me?

Well, I'll Tell You!

by Trisha Tester (ttester@earthlink.net)

Please allow me to introduce myself. I am a metastatic breast cancer patient. Although this means that I am almost certainly going to die of this disease (barring a miracle), I am not a victim. I don't like that word, and I would prefer that you never use that word around me. I am a regular person, who happened to be standing in the wrong place at the wrong time, and I got whacked with the cancer stick. I have noticed that people don't always know what to say to me any more, or what to do to help. Most people are loving, caring souls who really do want to help, but really have no clue what I need. To try to help you help me, I have made a list. Please keep in mind that this is purely a subjective list. I have tried to include other viewpoints, but I don't want you to think that all things work for all people. We are wonderfully, excitingly unique human beings. And so, of course, our needs will be different. You will have to judge which suggestions you feel would be appropriate, and what you would be comfortable with.

1. If I want to talk to you about what life will be like after I am dead, DO NOT under any circumstances give me that fake, terrified, cheerful smile and say "Oh don't talk like that. You will be fine." There is every likelihood that I will NOT be fine, and it is very comforting to me to know that you will tell stories of me to your children (AND MY CHILDREN), and will always hold me in your heart. It is incredibly comforting to hear that you will include my children, who are much too young to lose their mother, in your life in a much greater way than now while I am still here for them. You can not depress me, by acknowledg-

ing that death is probable or even imminent. I am all too aware of it. As a matter of fact, if you put on that fake cheer, all you are telling me is that you are not able to be "there" for me for MY needs. If that is the case (and I won't fault you if it is), don't even try to pretend. Just give me a quick hug (there is nothing about me that is contagious), and tell me you care, and skedaddle. I don't have the time to waste on fair weather friends.

2. Don't give me the standard offer, "If there's anything I can do for you, please don't hesitate to give me a call." Most of us are used to being strong and capable people, who have taken care of ourselves (and usually others) for decades. It is very uncomfortable to be in a position of not being able to do for ourselves. I would suggest that you drop in for a visit, pick up a broom, and sweep. Ask me if I have any plans for dinner, and just start making it. I won't ask you to do these things. I am not used to asking for help. I am not good at it. If it is an emergency, I will call out for help. But if it is the little day to day crap that piles up until it feels like it is going to consume me, I will probably not ask for your help. But I will be eternally grateful if you just come and do it. And ignore my "pooh-poohing" you away from it. Be assertive. (But never mean!)

3. Talk about old times often. This has come as a surprise to many people when I have suggested it to them. They say "But Aunt Nellie will think that I think she is about to die if I talk about old times." HELLO!! She IS about to die. I am about to die (although I hope it is prolonged by long periods of relative wellness). And I LOVE reminiscing. It helps me to remember fabulous times in my life that I may have forgotten. It brings me a smile. It helps me to remember that even if my life is cut much shorter than planned, that it has still been a GOOD life. It gives me a better sense of wholeness.

4. (Actually, corollary to 3.) Take some time to organize the photos into albums. I don't know a person alive (well, maybe one) who is really on top of their photos. Put everything else aside, and devote however much time it takes. Get the photos in albums, with captions, and stories. If you have a videocam, just set it up and let it go. If you just have a tape recorder, that would be great too. Not only will your loved one

have a superb walk down memory lane, generations to come will bless you. If I had only done this with my mother..........

5. Don't ever, EVER feel guilty for enjoying life. When you find yourself having a great time, and you happen to think of me, do NOT feel bad - not even for a microsecond. Life is short. For all of us, whether we live to be 10 or 105. Enjoy the hell out of it. I would if I were in your shoes. Heck, I do now. My favorite cliche du jour: Your life is a bag of coins to be spent any way you choose. But you can only spend it once. (Spend it wisely, my friends.)

6. Don't be afraid to be afraid. If you are paralyzed with fear (and believe me, I have been there - as has my family!) it's ok to tell me that you are afraid that I am going to die. I am afraid too. Sharing that fear really does in some way make it easier to handle. Denying it seems very very false. I need real. I have no use for false. Once we have shared the fear, amazingly enough, we can set it in back of us again and move on. If we don't do that, it will block our paths at every turn.

7. Chances are that my bills are a pile of unorganized paperwork in a box somewhere. Cancer is an incredibly overwhelmingly expensive proposition. All the charges are mindboggling, and intricate. Insurance companies (in my experience) are incompetent and potentially fraudulent bozos who screw up all the time. I don't know if they could really be that incompetent, or if perhaps they are encouraged to be so, hoping that you will throw up your hands in confusion and pay some of the things that they "forgot" to pay. At any rate, I would be enormously grateful if you would come by some day, without judgement as to what kind of a mess I have made of the pile, and help me straighten it out. Maybe make a few phone calls. Maybe write a few letters. You wouldn't believe what a difference it would make.

8. Say, "I love you" a lot. Depending on who you are, that may come out as "You are the funniest person I have ever met," or "In the history of mankind, there will never be another person as _____ as you," or simply "I love you". But this is your chance. Don't blow it. After a certain point, there is no going back for a makeup credit.

9. Be very conservative in what perfumes/colognes you wear. Chemo-therapy often makes for incredibly sensitive olfactory senses. Perfumes can be overwhelming and nauseating. I can't even sit next to my daughter when she eats a COLD sandwich. (No, not egg salad or tuna either). And by the same token, be especially sensitive if you are a smoker. (Unless the patient is a smoker - I wouldn't know about that situation.) If you do have to smoke, please go outside. Even if I say it is OK. And hang out outside for an extra 5 or 10 minutes to air out. You wouldn't believe how much vile aroma clings to you.

10. Make plans, not offers. Instead of asking if I want to do lunch sometime, ask me if next Tuesday is free. Then tell me, "Great! I will be by to pick you up at 11 so we can go out to lunch. Maybe we could do a little window-shopping if you are up to it." Of course, you will have to be flexible, in case Tuesday is one of those days that I feel like I have been run over by a huge truck......

11. When you ask me how I am, please remember that I am much more than my disease. I know that people ask out of concern, but I get a little tired of reciting disease progression/regression, treatment updates, symptom itemization, etc. Remember that we really did have things we used to talk about BEFORE I got whacked. Those things are still important to me.

12. Please be aware that "looking good" has NOTHING TO DO WITH IT. Don't worry - I even do it myself - tell my friends how good they look as if it meant that the cancer must be under control........ No such luck. Until the very very end stages, cancer itself frequently doesn't cause you any distress at all. Usually doesn't hurt. Often you can't even feel it (which is why so many of them go undetected for so long.) The treatments, on the other hand, can make you WANT to die. Even when they are saving or at least prolonging your life. This doesn't mean I want you to stop telling me I look good. I just want you to realize that it really doesn't mean diddly-squat.

13. I need you to realize that this experience has changed me in several ways. I am still the person I have always been, but I am different, too. For one thing, I am TIRED. You know how tired you are when you are sick? Imagine having that be your new "normal". Be sensitive to my

need to rest often. And don't expect me to be able to go as long or as fast as I used to do. I also don't have the memory I used to. Treatment has taken things from me that I will never get back. Now I feel like I am slogging through marshmallow goop, both physically AND mentally. Another change is in attitude. Some things just don't seem important to me any more. (Hopefully, I don't yell at my kids QUITE as much.) And other things have become more important. I talk to more strangers now. When I have something to say, I say it! It can be a little disconcerting. If I embarrass you, you are free to walk away and pretend you don't know me. But please don't try to limit me. Let me spend the rest of my life doing exactly what I want to do!

14. Go to the doctor's appointments with me. Sometimes my poor "chemo brain" drops important information. It is very companionable to have someone with me in the various waiting rooms (maybe someday doctors will operate in a timely fashion.......nah, never mind –it'll never happen!). And it's great to have someone to talk to during an infusion drip. It is a good idea to have a pre-written list of questions. Again, a tape recorder can come in handy. And if the doctor is a little short or brusque, dig your heels in and be assertive. Help me to remember that although I am but one file in the doctor's toppling stack of workload, I am the single most qualified protector of MY LIFE. I have every right to as much of the doctor's time as I need. He (in my case she) certainly keeps ME waiting long enough!

15. (Actually, corollary to 14.) If I don't like the doctor's advice, or manner, remind me that there are plenty of doctors out there, and I deserve a second (or third....) opinion. Cancer treatment - especially for metastatic disease, is not even close to refined yet. There is so much "art" and doctor's judgement to it, that I should never be coerced into a treatment I don't feel right about.

16. Respect my decision. There may come a time in this journey that I decide to lay down beside the road and stop fighting. If I make this choice, I know that you will be disappointed and dismayed. Maybe even furious. Please remember that it is my battle, and my decision. I know that you love me. I know that you want me to fight. But if that day ever comes, please understand that there is simply no more fight left. I promise you that I will never ever make that decision lightly.

17. If I am walking around bald from chemo, take the plunge. Shave your head! You would be surprised how refreshing it is to stick your head under a faucet on a hot summer day… Don't worry. I will not be in the least surprised if you "pass" on this suggestion. I can say in all honesty, I doubt if I would do it for you!

I hope that these suggestions help you to understand what is TRULY helpful, in dealing with a friend or loved one who is battling a life-threatening illness. Of course, the most important thing you can do is to just BE THERE. Listen. Perhaps your heart will hear what needs to be said or done. Bless you for caring, and may there be miracles for all of us.

March 2001

Well, February sped right on by without giving me the opportunity to update this page. With 3 school aged children and a full time job, you do what you have to do....which is usually what the kids want to do. That meant my oldest taking driver's ed and my daughter getting braces. Now whoever imagined that braces would become vogue?

Health wise, I guess I am ok. My 27-29 was 38 last month, up from 33 but it's the trend that matters. My bone scan was unremarkable and other than aches from the Aredia, I seem to tolerate the Aredia and Arimidex well. I take vitamins as well and have just recently added Indole -3-carbinol (I3C) to the mix as a test. I3C is a phytochemical isolated from cruciferous vegetables like broccoli and green cabbage. According to studies reported on the Life Extension Foundation website and in their "Disease Prevention and Treatment" book, I3C has modes of action similar to tamoxifen. It is reported to stop human cancer cells from growing and to provoke the cells to self destruct in what is known as apoptosis. I didn't know this but there appears to be more than one type of estrogen. The stronger form is estradiol and the weaker is estriol. Reportedly, I3C induces the body to convert the stronger form of estrogen into the weaker form. Estrogen just didn't seem to be a friend to me, thus the treatment of tamoxifen and the removal of my ovaries, and now Arimidex, so I3C may benefit me. We'll see.

I've also been reading books by Barbara Johnson. This next quote from one of her books is just so inspiring to me.

Stick a Geranium in Your Hat and Be Happy
Barbara Johnson

"How Do You Define 'Hope'?

Sometimes it's hard to explain hope---just what is hope, anyway? The cutest illustration of hope I've found is about a little boy who was standing at the foot of the escalator in a big department store, intently watching the handrail. He never took his eyes off the handrail as the escalator kept going around and around. A salesperson saw him and finally asked him if he was lost. The little boy replied, "Nope, I'm just waiting for my chewing gum to come back."
If your face is in the dust, if you are in a wringer situation, be like the little boy, waiting for his chewing gum to come back. Stand firm, be patient, and trust God. Then get busy with your life....there is work to do.
...nothing touches me that has not passed through the hands of my heavenly Father, NOTHING. Whatever occurs, God has sovereignly surveyed and approved. We may not know why (we may never know why), but we do know our pain is no accident to Him who guides our lives. He is, in no way, surprised by it all. Before it ever touches us, it passes through Him."

WOW! I have asked the question a time or two about 'why me?' "Why do I have cancer?" I think we all ask a similar question in our life. It's an awesome thought for me to know that God has looked at the cancer long before I ever got it and has approved me for it. I believe I can handle it if He has surveyed and put his stamp of approval on it.

Till next time!!!

APRIL 2001

Welcome to Spring!!!!! I love this time of year. I hope this month finds you all doing well and enjoying the longer days and warmer weather.

It's been yet another busy time for us. Since I last updated, we have actually done a lot. (My English teacher hated those words--she said they are not descriptive) Ok, so I am about to describe what A LOT has been for me and my family.

March 27-28: Eddie and I went down to Brooke Army Medical Center (BAMC) to have my port put in. Eddie and I made good use of the two days (one for preop--the other for the port) by visiting the San Antonio Riverwalk and the Alamo. We had the best time and although it rained, the riverwalk was still an awesome experience. My port placement went well although after it was placed and I was getting ready to leave, my heart did some weird sort of fluttering but an xray and ekg showed things fine. We thought perhaps the fluttering might be from all the drugs given for the procedure.

March 30: Chris turned 16!!!! My smallest baby of the three is my physically largest child and is now on his way to beginning life as an adult. He got his driver's license that day and the keys to the Thunderbird. How fast they grow.

April 1: Eddie and I are graciously given two tickets to the Texas Motor Speedway to see the NASCAR race. Mark Martin is our family favorite driver. What an awesome experience to see our favorite driver zip around the track and listen to he and his crew while they fight the powerful track for 500 miles. I will never watch a race on TV the same after seeing the real thing. It was just incredible and I am forever indebted to those gracious people who gave us the tickets.

April 4-6: I wake up at 3:00 a.m. to fluttering in my chest that continued for hours. I had experienced off and on fluttering since the port placement, however this was really scarey! It wouldn't stop. I went to my local military treatment facility and had an ekg which I guess wasn't the best or worst. So they gave me a 24 hour holter type monitor to wear. I went back the next day and dropped it off, then on Friday morning had a lateral xray of the chest. Next thing I know, I am back down to BAMC having the port repositioned so it will quit making my heart appear to flutter. I found out during that experience that some IV drugs contain Sulfa as a preservative as I reacted to the two antibiotic IV drugs they gave me. The good news is, the port is fixed! I had it accessed yesterday (4/20) for my Aredia treatment and blood draw and it worked well! Less traumatic than digging for a usable vein in my one good arm. WHEW!

April 14: Through Making Memories Org. and on air personalities at a Dallas radio station, KYNG, my family and I spent the day with Team Texas and the only word that comes to mind to adequately describe our day is AWESOME!!!!! Eddie drove a REAL Winston Cup Car and me and the kids got driven around the Texas Motor Speeway in a real Cup car! It was an incredible day! We also met Eric Norris who is such a GENUINE heart. He talked with us and rode around the track in a van with us while "Hippy" showed Eddie his marks to look for upon getting behind the wheel of the Cup car. I am not good at names, but I thank Whitey, Mr. Stone (the photographer), Mike, Hippy, Mr. Norris, and all the people out at the track that day who made one family an incredible memory!

April 17: Again, as part of Making Memories Org. and those who volunteered their good will, I got a very sweet phone call from my favorite Nascar Driver.... Mark Martin. I was at work and we didn't talk long but Mr. Martin was very kind to take a few moments out of his already busy day to call me. What a cherished phone call.....and I thank you Mr. Martin!!!! Good luck at Talladega this week!

Well, I am going to leave you this month with some thoughts I have pondered over the past few weeks. It has been a year since I found out about the cancer being back. Below is a post I made to Friends In Need and I encourage you to email me at trace@n-link.com to share what God has done in your life:

I've been sort of reflecting on the past year as of late. This time last year all the tests were being run to determine if the cancer was back and it was an incredibly frightening time. Eddie had to come back from Korea and it was like a dark veil was thrown around my head.

So, what's that have to do with now? Well yesterday, I am sitting out back reading and just stop to look around, listen to the birds, and watch the trees move with the breeze. Eddie comes out and says, "I thought you were reading" I say, "I was but I was thinking on this last year"

I pose a question to him as I did my MIL last night and I am really posing it to God but will say it out loud to see if any of ya'll have been where I am. (I am sure you all have)

This past year has gone by so fast, but looking back, have I grown mentally and most importantly, have I grown spiritually? This time last year, I remember thinking and begging God, "NO, I don't want to die" And I guess I can answer the spiritual question by saying I have grown a little as I hopped in a car doing 160 mph with no fear about anything including dying.

But how did I get here? And how much further do I have to go? Can I tell you what God has shared with my heart in the past year? The first thing that I have accepted is that this cancer is His will for my life. And if it's His will, how can I be against it? And as stupid as it sounds, I wouldn't change a thing. Don't get me wrong, I don't wish I had cancer, but I do and if I had to do it over, I would do it again. I'm not the same me as before and I like this me better. YIKES!

I've also learned that today is truly that proverbial GIFT. It's mine and I can't give it away and if I don't use it, it's wasted and I don't get it back. WHOA! WHAT A CONCEPT. And once I learned and accepted that, I learned to STAY IN TODAY.

I only have the strength to take each day at a time. And bust it down if I need to ...one hour at a time, one second at a time. When I shared this thought with my friend Angela, I said, "stay in this second".....she had another take on what I said. She interpreted that phrase as "stay in this– second" meaning let God lead. And how true and how I have adopted that as a heart truth.

I've also learned through Barbara Johnson books that one needs JOY. Now we've all heard that JOY means Jesus, Others, You. I have accepted this as a heart truth. And I look for JOY everyday. I try and sometimes struggle to find the 'upside' to everything. If's it's a long line at the grocery store, then the upside is that I am able to stand in that line, or able to converse with the person in front or behind me. If it's heavy traffic, then it's an opportunity to listen to music, pray, or sit in silence. You get the idea.

I'm struggling with humility. Some say, "I could never do what you do" and it's easy to put the focus on me but you know what, IT'S NOT ME.

It's HIM. My strength comes from the Lord and without HIM I would be a pile of jello. (And green at that...ugh) Angela said to me the other day when I mentioned that struggle, and she said, "YOU have a problem with humility?" Yes, because the ME wants to come out so many times. I had a bad attitude the other day when something didn't go my way and I let if effect my attitude. It wasn't until a day or two later (YIKES, I'm slow) that I turned it over to God, that I was able to let it go.

I know this is a novel but guys, I guess first, I wanted to share what this past year has been like in dealing with metastatic disease, and second, I would like to know your heart truths. I believe we can uplift each other in sharing our hearts, whether it's truths or fears. I can say now, and I couldn't say it last year with honesty, "Lord, I don't want to die, but if it's your will, take me on home" Can I hear from you guys?

And notice I didn't get into if I have grown mentally.....LOL

Have a great day.

MAY 2001

OK, SO I AM JUST A LITTLE LATE IN WRITING MY UPDATE....BUT WHAT A WONDERFUL MONTH IT HAS BEEN.

WE STARTED OUT THE MONTH GOING UP TO DALLAS TO WATCH THE FILMING OF "THE PRESIDENT'S MAN." THIS IS GOING TO BE A MOVIE OF THE WEEK PROBABLY TO BE RELEASED IN OCTOBER. WHAT A THRILL IT WAS TO GO UP THERE AND WATCH THE MAKING OF A MOVIE!! I NEVER KNEW SO MUCH WENT INTO ENTERTAINING US. ERIC

NORRIS INVITED US UP AND I HAVE TO SAY THIS ABOUT ERIC, THAT BOY HAS SO MUCH ENERGY!!! HE SHOULD BOTTLE IT UP AND SELL IT...HE WOULD MAKE A MINT!!! (NOT TO MENTION, I WOULD BUY SOME TO IMPROVE MY ENERGY LEVEL..OR BETTER YET, THE LACK THEREOF.) ERIC SHOWED ME AND MY FAMILY AN INCREDIBLE DAY COMPLETE WITH THE EXPLODING OF A CAR. I HAVE PHOTOS OF THIS, HOWEVER MY BRAND NEW SCANNER IS NOT WORKING.....(MAYBE IT'S THE OPERATOR? LOL). I HOPE TO HAVE IT FIXED SOON.

NOT ONLY WAS ERIC WONDERFUL TO US, HIS FATHER, CHUCK NORRIS WAS JUST AS WONDERFUL. (LIKE FATHER-LIKE SON?) MR. NORRIS WAS EVER SO PATIENT TO US EXPLAINING THE STUNTS AND HE TREATED US, NOT AS GUESTS, BUT AS HIS FRIEND. FOR AS MUCH AS THE NORRIS FAMILY DOES, THEY APPEAR TO BE VERY LAID BACK!!! NOT LIKE YOU WOULD EXPECT SOMEONE OF A 'CELEBRITY' STATUS TO BE. I LOOK AT THE 'WALKER TEXAS RANGER' CHARACTER NOW AND SEE THAT HE IS NOT REALLY A CHARACTER, BUT TRULY AN EXAMPLE OF THE TRUE CHUCK NORRIS. AGAIN, I HAVE PICTURES, BUT....GRRRRRRRR......I NEED TO GET THIS SCANNER FIXED!

MY DAUGHTER KATY CELEBRATED HER 13TH BIRTHDAY BY GETTING HER HAIR HIGHLIGHTED. YOU COULDN'T HAVE ASKED FOR A HAPPIER LITTLE LADY. DOING MOTHER DAUGHTER THINGS THESE DAYS IS LIKE HAVING A BEST FRIEND TO ME. I JUST LOVE HER AGE AND I HOPE AS SHE HAS A DAUGHTER OF HER OWN, SHE WILL LOOK BACK AT THE SPECIALS TIMES WE HAD AND WANT TO SHARE THAT WITH HER OWN.

THE KIDS ARE OUT OF SCHOOL FOR THE SUMMER. LAST YEAR THEY WENT TO CONNECTICUT. THIS YEAR THEY WILL HAVE TO STAY HERE. FINDING THINGS TO KEEP

THREE SCHOOL AGED CHILDREN BUSY AND CHALLENGED IS GOING TO BE A STRUGGLE FOR ME AS ABOUT THE TIME THEY GET WOUND UP, I'M READY TO DROP.

WHICH BRINGS ME TO MY WORK DECISION. I LOVE MY WORK BUT I HAVE FOUND LATELY THAT I DON'T HAVE THE STAMINA I USE TO. (OLD AGE AT 38?) I HAVE MADE A PROPOSAL TO MY BOSS THAT I PHASE IN THIS MONTH WORKING THREE DAYS IN THE OFFICE AND TWO DAYS AT HOME. I WANT IT TO WORK AND MANY PEOPLE TELECOMMUTE, SO I AM HOPING FOR A SUCCESSFUL RUN AT WORKING WHILE HAVING METS. THIS PAST YEAR HAS WORKED OUT BUT I AM READY TO SLOW DOWN NOW. IF ANY OF YOU HAVE EXPERIENCE IN TELECOMMUTING, I'M ALL EARS.

MEDICALLY, PRAISE GOD, I AM STABLE. (MENTALLY? LOL) I'M HANGING STEADY AND HOPE AND PRAY THAT THIS TREND CONTINUES.

JULY 2001

WELCOME TO JULY!!!! I HAVE INCLUDED THIS BEAUTIFUL GLOBE CREATED BY PATSI AND YOU CAN VISIT HER SITE BY CLICKING ON THE GLOBE! THANK YOU PATSI FOR ALLOWING ME TO USE YOUR BEAUTIFUL WORK!

IT'S BEEN A BUSY TIME AS USUAL FOR OUR FAMILY. WE BEGAN THE MONTH OF JUNE BY GOING TO THE TEXAS MOTOR SPEEDWAY TO WATCH ERIC NORRIS RACE IN THE

NASCAR CRAFTSMAN TRUCK SERIES. HE DID NOT WIN THE RACE BUT WAS STILL A WINNER IN MY EYES. HE BEGAN THE RACE DEAD LAST AND FINISHED 17TH. IT WAS AN AWESOME EXPERIENCE TO WATCH HIM AND HIS TEAM WORK SO HARD. HE IS GOING TO GO FAR IN THE RACING WORLD!

NEXT MY DAUGHTER AND I WENT TO AUSTIN TO MEET UP WITH ERIN FROM THE FRIENDS IN NEED SITE. I HAD THE MOST INCREDIBLE TIME! WE TOURED THE STATE CAPITAL, SHOPPED, AND SPENT TWO DAYS GETTING TO KNOW EACH OTHER. ERIN AND HER FRIENDS ARE WONDERFUL LADIES! WE TRIED OUT THIS CAJOUN RESTAURANT AND LITTLE MISS ERIN ATE RAW OYSTERS! YIKES! WHAT A BRAVE WOMAN! SHE ALSO INTRODUCED ME TO THE WORLD OF COMFORTABLE SHOES! LORD KNOWS I HAVE ENOUGH TROUBLE WITH MY FEET. I CERTAINLY NEED THE MOST COMFORTABLE SHOES I CAN GET. :-) THANK YOU ERIN! AT THAT RESTAURANT WE WERE OFFERED BEADS SUCH AS THOSE AT MARDIGRAS. I OF COURSE WANTED THE PINK ONES. DORKY ME FELL ASLEEP WITH MY BEADS ON AND WOKE UP THE NEXT MORNING WITH A PINK NECK. SORT OF RUINS MY REPUTATION AS A FIRST CLASS REDNECK. :-)

I RECENTLY HAD MY BONE SCAN. THERE SEEMS TO BE NEW AREAS OF 'UPTAKE' HOWEVER I AM NOT CONCERNED ABOUT IT. THROUGH MY MANY TRAVELS ON THE NET, I LEARNED THAT HAVING AREDIA TOO CLOSE TO A BONE SCAN CAN PRODUCE A FALSE POSITIVE. I DON'T THINK A WEEK HAD PASSED FROM MY AREDIA TREATMENT TO THE BONE SCAN. THE REASON A FALSE POSITIVE CAN HAPPEN IS DUE TO THE FOLLOWING EXPLANATION FROM ANOTHER LIST I READ.

Here's why that happens. When you get a bone scan you receive an injection of a bisphosphonate that is laced with a radioactive material.

The bisphosphonate is drawn to areas of activity or injury in the bone. The radioactive material allows this to be seen on the scan. ...... And AREDIA is another bisphosphonate. It strengthens bones and helps prevent fractures because it is drawn to activity and injury in the bone. An Aredia infusion followed too quickly by a scan can show uptake in areas that are not bone mets or injury. The Aredia rep suggested at least a week after an infusion before getting a scan.

AN INTERESTING CONCEPT. WE WILL HANG OUT AND RETEST AGAIN IN A COUPLE OF MONTHS, HOWEVER I'LL TRY TO HAVE THE BONE SCAN LIKE A DAY BEFORE MY AREDIA TREATMENT SO AS NOT TO CAUSE ANY CONFUSION.

ON MANY LISTS THERE ARE MAJOR AND ENLIGTENING DISCUSSIONS ABOUT A POSSIBLE LINK BETWEEN WEIGHT GAIN AND CHEMO. THAT SUBJECT IS NEAR AND DEAR TO MY HEART AS SINCE THE REMOVAL OF MY OVARIES LAST YEAR, I HAVE PUT ON ALMOST 20 POUNDS. AT THIS RATE, I COULD BECOME A PROFESSIONAL WRESTLER IN NO TIME. :-) TO COMBAT THE WEIGHT GAIN AND HOPEFULLY IMPROVE FATIGUE, I HAVE INSTITUTED A DAILY WALKING ROUTINE INTO MY ALREADY BUSY DAY. I AM SEEING IMMEDIATE RESULTS, NOT IN WEIGHT REDUCTION, BUT IN ENERGY LEVELS. I FEEL BETTER ALREADY WITH ONLY WALKING AT LEAST ONE MILE EACH DAY. I KNOW IT'S AN UPHILL BATTLE TRYING TO FIGHT MIDDLE AGE, SURGICAL MENTAL-PAUSE, THE LOVE OF FOOD, AND DRUGS TO FIGHT OFF THE CANCER, BUT HEY, IT DOESN'T HURT TO TRY, RIGHT?

WELL, ENOUGH OF THE GABBING. BE GOOD TO YOURSELVES AND I'LL TRY TO GET ALL THESE NEW PICTURES ONLINE. UNTIL NEXT TIME........

SEPTEMBER 11, 2001

DO IT AGAIN, LORD by Max Lucado

Dear Lord,

We're still hoping we'll wake up. We're still hoping we'll open a sleepy eye and think, "What a horrible dream."

But we won't, will we, Father? What we saw was not a dream. Planes did gouge towers. Flames did consume our fortress. People did perish. It was no dream and, dear Father, we are sad.

There is a ballet dancer who will no longer dance and a doctor who will no longer heal. A church has lost her priest, a classroom is minus a teacher.

Cora ran a food pantry. Paige was a counselor and Dana, dearest Father, Dana was only three years old. (Who held her in those final moments?)

We are sad, Father. For as the innocent are buried, our innocence is buried as well. We thought we were safe. Perhaps we should have known better. But we didn't.

And so we come to you. We don't ask you for help; we beg you for it. We
don't request it; we implore it. We know what you can do. We've read the
accounts. We've pondered the stories and now we plead, "Do it again, Lord.
Do it again."

Remember Joseph? You rescued him from the pit. You can do the same for us.
Do it again, Lord.

Remember the Hebrews in Egypt? You protected their children from the angel
of death. We have children too, Lord. Do it again.

And Sarah? Remember her prayers? You heard them. Joshua? Remember his
fears? You inspired him. The women at the tomb? You resurrected their
hope. The doubts of Thomas? You took them away. Do it again, Lord. Do it
again.

You changed Daniel from a captive into a king's counselor. You took Peter
the fisherman and made him Peter an apostle. Because of you, David went
from leading sheep to leading armies. Do it again, Lord, for we need
counselors today, Lord. We need apostles. We need leaders. Do it again,
dear Lord.

Most of all, do again what you did at Calvary. What we saw here last Tuesday, you saw there that Friday. Innocence slaughtered. Goodness murdered. Mothers weeping. Evil dancing. Just as the smoke eclipsed out
morning, so the darkness fell on your Son. Just as our towers were shattered, the very Tower of Eternity was pierced. And by dusk, heaven's
sweetest song was silent, buried behind a rock. But you did not waver, O
Lord. You did not waver. After three days in a dark hole, you rolled the rock and rumbled the earth and turned the darkest Friday into the brightest Sunday. Do it again, Lord, Grant us a September Easter.

We thank you, dear Father, for these hours of unity. Christians are praying with Jews. Republicans are standing with Democrats. Skin colors have been
covered by the ash of burning buildings. We thank you for these hours of
unity.

And we thank you for these hours of prayer. The Enemy sought to bring us
to our knees and succeeded. He had no idea, however, that we would kneel
before you. And he has no idea what you can do.

Let your mercy be upon our President, Vice President, and their families.
Grant to those who lead us wisdom beyond their years and experience. Have
mercy upon the souls who have departed and the wounded who remain. Give us grace that we might forgive and faith that we might believe.

And look kindly upon your church. For two thousand years you've used her to heal a hurting world.

DO IT AGAIN LORD, DO IT AGAIN.
Through Christ,
Amen.

NOVEMBER 2001

HAPPY THANKSGIVING EVERYONE! I HOPE YOU HAD AN
ENJOYABLE DAY FILLED WITH LOVE, FAMILY, FOOD, AND
OF COURSE THAT AFTER-MEAL NAP.
I DIDN'T UPDATE LAST MONTH SINCE NOTHING NEW
REGARDING MY HEALTH HAD OCCURED AND SINCE I WAS
BUSY SPENDING A WONDERFUL WEEK IN VIRGINIA
VISITING FAMILY AND FRIENDS. WORDS CAN'T EXPRESS
THE JOY FELT DURING THAT WEEK AND I REALIZE THAT I
CAN'T LET ANOTHER THREE YEARS GO BEFORE I VISIT
AGAIN.

AND WHILE I SPENT TIME IN NEWPORT NEWS, VIRGINIA WE
TOOK A DAY TRIP UP TO BUENA VISTA TO VISIT MY
GRAMMA'S SISTER, GERRY, AND HER FAMILY. THE
MOUNTAINS WERE BEAUTIFUL AND THE COLORS, OH THE
COLORS.....SOMETHING THIS PART OF TEXAS SIMPLY DOES
NOT GET THE OPPORTUNITY TO ENJOY.

THE LAST NIGHT I SPENT IN VIRGINIA, WE HAD A GOOD
TIME AT MY GPARENT'S HOUSE EATING PIZZA AND
CRACKING ON EACH OTHER. TO ME, IT WAS LIKE
CHRISTMAS IN OCTOBER.

I CAME BACK TO TEXAS TO FIND OUT THAT MY TUMOR
MARKER CA27-29 IS ON THE RISE AGAIN AFTER A YEAR OF
GOOD RESULTS. WHAT DOES THAT MEAN? I DON'T KNOW.

WHAT I DO KNOW IS THAT SINCE I HAVE BEEN ON THE ARIMIDEX FOR OVER A YEAR, WE HAVE NOW SWITCHED TO A DRUG CALLED FEMARA. I JUST STARTED FEMARA THREE DAYS AGO. IN THE NEXT COUPLE OF WEEKS WE WILL BE DOING SCANS AND STUFF TO SEE IF THE RISING TUMOR MARKER IS A FLUKE OR SOMETHING TO GET ANXIOUS ABOUT. SINCE I LOOK WELL AND FEEL WELL, WE ARE JUST GOING TO LET THIS PLAY OUT. IF IT IS THE CANCER ON THE MOVE AGAIN, PERHAPS THE FEMARA CAN BACK IT UP AGAIN JUST LIKE THE ARIMIDEX DID. YOUR CONTINUED PRAYERS ARE APPRECIATED.

MARCH 2002

IT HAS BEEN QUITE SOME TIME SINCE I HAVE UPDATED. MANY THINGS HAVE HAPPENED REGARDING THE CANCER SITUATION. IN NOVEMBER WE FOUND OUT THAT MY TUMOR MARKER WAS RISING AND WE DROPPED THE ARIMIDEX AND BEGAN FEMARA. A BONE SCAN AND MRI SHOWED THE BONE METS WERE INCREASING IN THE LOWER HIP AREA AND IN JANUARY I HAD 10 ROUNDS OF RADIATION. AFTER TAKING THE FEMARA, HAVING RADIATION AND THE MARKER STILL CONTINUED TO RISE, WE QUIT THE DRUG AND I AM NOW WAITING ON MY PRESCRIPTION FOR AROMASIN. FASLODEX IS DUE TO BECOME APPROVED BY THE FDA SOON BUT AS OF THIS WRITING IT HAS NOT RECEIVED APPROVAL. UNLIKE ARIMIDEX, FEMARA, AND AROMASIN, FASLODEX IS A ONCE A MONTH INJECTION.

I BELIEVE EACH OF THE ABOVE DRUGS ARE CONSIDERED HORMONAL THERAPIES OR AROMATASE INHIBITORS. THEY EACH WORK DIFFERENTLY IN THE BODY IN THAT

TAMOXIFEN BLOCKS ESTROGEN FROM ESTROGEN RECEPTORS IN BREAST CANCER; ARIMIDEX PREVENTS PRODUCTION OF ESTROGEN IN ADRENAL GLANDS; FASLODEX DESTROYS ESTROGEN RECEPTORS IN BREAST CANCER CELLS. I AM NOT SURE HOW THAT ALL MAKES A DIFFERENCE IN TREATMENT I CAN TELL YOU THAT TAMOXIFEN HELD ME IN REMISSION FOR 5 YEARS AND ARIMIDEX FOR ABOUT 18 MONTHS.

BESIDES THE HEALTH SITUATION, WE ALL CONTINUE TO DO WELL. THE KIDS EACH HAVE THEIR RESPECTIVE DEALS AT SCHOOL THEY ARE INVOLVED IN. EDDIE IS LOOKING FORWARD TO PUTTING IN HIS RETIREMENT PACKET AND I CUT MY WORK HOURS TO PART TIME TO CONCENTRATE ON IMPROVING MY HEALTH.

ONE OF THE MAJOR ISSUES I AM LOOKING INTO NOW IS PAIN MANAGEMENT. I CANNOT IMAGINE THAT BONEY METS WOULD BE PAIN FREE AND FROM SOME OF THE PAIN I HAVE HAD RECENTLY, IT SEEMS REASONABLE THAT I SHOULD GAIN CONTROL OVER THE PAIN NOW AND NOT WAIT UNTIL MY SITUATION TURNS SERIOUS. IN READING UP ON PAIN MANAGEMENT, I FIND THAT A LOT OF PATIENTS ARE LIKE ME. SOME UNDERSTATE THEIR PAIN. MOST PHYSICIANS NOW USE A NUMBERED SCALE BUT WHY DO I STILL UNDERESTIMATE MY ACTUAL PAIN TO MY ONCOLOGIST? TO BE FRANK, I DON'T KNOW. IT'S JUST AS WEIRD AS I AM. I DO NOT BELIEVE THERE IS SUCH A THING AS PAIN MED "JUNKIES" WHEN DEALING WITH METS PAIN. I MEAN, PERSONALLY, MY GOAL IS TO STOP THE HURT, NOT SEE HOW HIGH I CAN GET. PLUS, I CANNOT REMEMBER THE LAST TIME A PAIN MED HAD A EUPHORIC EFFECT ON ME....DARN! :-) BUT FOR THE LIFE OF ME, WHY I CAN'T READILY SAY HOW PAIN OR NO PAIN IS IN MY LIFE NOW IS BEYOND ME. WHAT I CAN SAY IS THAT I PLAN TO GET A HEAD START ON CONTROLLING IT NOW BEFORE I FIND

MYSELF ONE DAY WISHING I HAD.

SO WITH ALL THAT SAID, I LEAVE YOU WITH IF YOU HAVE
NOT ALREADY DONE SO, PLEASE CHECK OUT THE NEW
PICTURES PAGES 3 AND 4. I AM NOT THE BEST AT PUTTING
TOGETHER A WEB PAGE OR EVEN PUTTING PICTURES UP
HERE BUT I THINK THEY CAME OUT CLEAR ENOUGH TO
DISTINQUISH WHO IS WHO.

UNTIL NEXT TIME

SEPTEMBER 2002

Wow, has it been a while since I have updated. I think I said the same
thing in March when updating. Suffice to say, many things have
changed since then. I am now off of the aromatase inhibitors and am
now on a drug called Xeloda. I am taking 1800 mgs twice a day for 14
days, then have 7 days off before I start a new cycle. I started this
chemo in April and my tumor marker has fallen from 451 to 207. I had
tremendous bone pain during that time and was taking morphine but am
happy to report that not only has there been a reduction in the tumor
marker, there has been a reduction in pain. I no longer take the morphine.

Xeloda was a tremendous help to me in June in that by being in pill
form, I was able to travel to Virginia when my Grandfather had to have
surgery. Being bound by iv infusions every three weeks as in standard
chemo, would have made the trip next to impossible. Instead I was
afforded the blessing of being around my family and supporting them
in their time of need. Besides the two surgeries my Grandfather had to
endure, it was still great fun being there.

I am back at work full time. This is something different to me in that earlier in the year, I felt I may just progress instead of work again towards remission. My energy is back to some degree and although I have some down days, I have more ups than downs. Guess that's the nature of this disease.

I'm back more into developing relationships. For a while I was afraid to reveal myself any more than necessary. Again, when one is in pain, it's hard to think in the light and I look at that time of pain as what was a dark period. But back to relationships....people are important to me. Their role in my life and my role in theirs. Relationships, and I mean, meaningful ones, mean more to me than any amount of money. Just the touch of a friend, or the look in the eyes of a loved one, speaks more to me than the volumes of books on this earth. And why do I think that? I think because whether I live 1 year or 100 more, the relationship I have with others will carry over to other generations. And the gift people give me by being a part of my life, is something I will carry with me through the rest of my life. Some things I can call up as reserve when I'm feeling down when I remember me and another acting goofy in a store. The memory may be a springboard to getting up out of the funk.

Truly, I don't make sense but if I make a little sense, I urge you to look at the relationships that you have in your life. Even the ones that look broken. Is there something that you can do that could change the day of a person or heal the wound of angry words. Can just a smile from you start a chain reaction that could reach around the world? Just think about it. And email me with any comments. I'm all ears these days!!!

Till next time.

Many blessings and hugz to you.

Your friend,

Trace

February 2003 update

As our country prepares to go to war with Iraq, I prepare to go to war once again with the cancer. After a successful run with the Xeloda, it had pretty much run its course and we had to change battle plans when hip pain led to the discovery of more widespread bone mets. Subsequent testing revealed no detectable soft tissue mets. With that knowledge we have completed more radiation to the hip area and because I am considered 'stable' we began Faslodex
last week. I would like to find the magic bullet to keep the bone mets at bay and I understand that people can live with breast cancer in the bones for years, but it seems the more it progresses, the more painful it is. Ugh. This too shall pass......and I'm still seeking a cure.

I've gone through many emotional painful trials since the last update and I have to believe that the trials will make me a better person when all is said and done. I do not feel like a better person when I am wallowing in my own pity and despair, however somehow the sun always comes out again and I look back and see how far I've come. It's then that I realize that now is not the time to give up. Now is the time to press on. Several of the ways the sun always comes out I lay out below:

Emilie Barnes has a book entitled "A
Cup of Hope-Resting in the Promise of God's Faithfulness." Emilie herself is a breast cancer survivor and she lays out some very good visuals that I currently rely on to get me through those pity and despair days. Even if you do not have breast cancer or metastatic disease, but are just struggling through a rough period in your life, I urge you to pick up this little book. It may be a little book but it is packed with a ton of spirit lifting words of encouragement for days when you feel there is no hope. She has a way of reminding you that

your God has not left you and He quietly stands there ready to take your hand to help you up. Thank you Emilie

Myolder sister has graciously given of her time and talent to take over my web page for me. I cannot begin to explain how much of a relief that is for me since I lack in the talent to put together something coherent in a timely fashion. I'm sure you, the reader, have noticed how spaced apart my updates are. It's simply because God didn't bless me with the internet talents He has given to my sister. My sister has also been an inspiration to me and a reminder to press on. When I am feeling down, I feel that she senses it and it's not a moment later that my phone starts ringing. I urge you that if you have a sister or someone in your life that represents a sister or sisterhood to give that person a call or a hug and tell them how much they mean to you and how much you love them. To my big sis~~I love ya sistah!

I have a couple of friends here in the town I live in who have given of themselves to me in ways that makes me think that they may be my long lost sisters or something too. Michelle has so much going on in her life right now and to be quite frank, more than anyone could ever want, however she always takes the time to pick up the phone and ask about me or just listen to me ramble about nothingness. Her 'no worries' comment always brings a giggle to me but yet, I believe in her heart she actually believes that circumstance is really a 'no worries' thing if we tackle it from a proper perspective. Go Michelle! I love ya sistah!

And then there is Patti. God gave Patti a heart as big as Texas. She has taken that big sister attitude with me and you had best bring several armies if you are going to mess with me, whether emotionally or physically. I think if cancer was a person, she would have wiped the floor with it a loong time ago. Thank you Patti for all that you do and know that I love ya sistah!

Finally, as my illness seems to progress here, I understand that I am so truly blessed. Blessed in more ways than I will ever know. I have loving family, friends, and newfound sisters in this journey we call life. I appreciate your prayers of support and healing and please know that they are never taken for granted. If metastatic cancer can be beat, I'm sure love has something to do with it.

Until next time......

Trace

"Today Lord, I thank you for the love I receive from the children you have blessed me with."